Parliamentary Reform in Britain, c. 1770–1918

ERIC J. EVANS

An imprint of PEARSON EDUCATION

Harlow, England · London · New York · Reading · Massachusetts · San Francisco ·
Toronto · Don Mills, Ontario · Sydney · Tokyo · Singapore · Hong Kong · Seoul ·
Taipei · Cape Town · Madrid · Mexico City · Amsterdam · Munich · Paris · Milan

328·41 EVA

153 364

Pearson Education Limited,
Edinburgh Gate,
Harlow,
Essex CM20 2JE,
United Kingdom
and Associated Companies throughout the world.

Visit us on the World Wide Web at:
www.pearsoned.co.uk

First published 2000

ISBN-10: 0-582-29467-3
ISBN-13: 978-0-582-29467-7

Visit our world wide web site at http://www.awl-he.com

British Library Cataloguing-in-Publication Data
A catalogue record for this book is available from the British Library

Library of Congress Cataloging-in-Publication Data
Evans, Eric J., 1945–
   Parliamentary reform, c1770-1918 / by Eric J. Evans.
   p.   cm. – (Seminar studies in history)
   Includes bibliographical references and index.
   ISBN 0-582-29467-3 (PPR)
   1. Great Britain. Parliament–Reform–History. I.Title.
II. Series.
JN521.E94   1999
328.41'070409034–dc21   99-20830
                                               CIP

8 7 6
09 08 07 06

Set by 7 in 10/12 Sabon
Printed in Malaysia, PPSB

CONTENTS

   IN THE DARK'   44
   Liberal Proposals and Liberal Opposition   44
   A Conservative Bill which did not Conserve   48

7. CONSEQUENCES: THE LEAP AND ITS AFTERMATH, 1867–80 55
   How Much Change?   55
   Political Organisations and Party Fortunes   58
   A Respectable Electorate?   61

8. CORRUPTION, REFORM AND REDISTRIBUTION, 1883–85   65
   Corruption   65
   Reform and Redistribution, 1884–85   68
   Consequences   70

   PART FOUR: VOTES FOR WOMEN – AND MANY MORE
   MEN   75

9. THE WOMEN'S SUFFRAGE CAMPAIGN, 1867–1914   75
   Images and Stereotypes   75
   Women and Local Politics   77
   The Liberal and Labour Parties   79
   Turning the Tide?   81

10. TOWARDS DEMOCRACY, 1910–18   83
    The House of Lords   83
    War and the Franchise   87
    Reform and Party Politics   89

    PART FIVE: CONCLUSION AND ASSESSMENT   91
    The Twentieth Century   91
    Safety in Numbers   93
    Empire, Progress and Myth   94

    PART SIX: DOCUMENTS   96
    Chronology   120
    Appendix I: Parliamentary Reform Legislation, 1832–1928   129
    Appendix II: The Growth of the Electorate as a Result of
    Parliamentary Reform, 1831–1929   136
    Bibliography   137
    Index   146

NOTE ON REFERENCING SYSTEM

Readers should note that numbers in square brackets [5] refer them to the corresponding entry in the Bibliography at the end of the book (specific page numbers are given in italics). A number in square brackets preceded by *Doc.* [*Doc. 5*] refers readers to the corresponding item in the Documents section which follows the main text.

AN INTRODUCTION TO THE SERIES

Such is the pace of historical enquiry in the modern world that there is an ever-widening gap between the specialist article or monograph, incorporating the results of current research, and general surveys, which inevitably become out of date. *Seminar Studies in History* are designed to bridge this gap. The series was founded by Patrick Richardson in 1966 and his aim was to cover major themes in British, European and World history. Between 1980 and 1996 Roger Lockyer continued his work, before handing the editorship over to Clive Emsley and Gordon Martel. Clive Emsley is Professor of History at the Open University, while Gordon Martel is Professor of International History at the University of Northern British Columbia, Canada and Senior Research Fellow at De Montfort University.

All the books are written by experts in their field who are not only familiar with the latest research but have often contributed to it. They are frequently revised, in order to take account of new information and interpretations. They provide a selection of documents to illustrate major themes and provoke discussion, and also a guide to further reading. The aim of *Seminar Studies* is to clarify complex issues without over-simplifying them, and to stimulate readers into deepening their knowledge and understanding of major themes and topics.

PART ONE: ORIGINS

1 PARLIAMENTARY REFORM AND THE HISTORIANS

CHANGING PERSPECTIVES ON REFORM

As in other aspects of life, fashions in historical writing change. Not so long ago, it was possible to write about parliamentary reform in the nineteenth and early twentieth centuries by concentrating on the Acts themselves. The causes of each would be dutifully considered, the terms written down in as much detail as the scope of the book required, and the consequences for political parties and other aspects of high politics analysed. In much of the early writing, also, the implicit (and sometimes explicit) assumption was that, in explaining the causes and consequences of parliamentary reform, one was also charting progress. The story revealed the emergence of a parliamentary democracy, as each Act extended the franchise and, in some way or other, made votes more equal and voting 'fairer'. It was perfectly possible to approach democracy by citing some of the key dates which are found in the chronology: 1832, 1867, 1872, 1883–85, 1918, 1928, and so on. Britain's advanced system of government, which guarantees that mechanisms exist for the peaceful and orderly transfer of power, emerged in stages and could be held up as an example to others.

At the height of Britain's power and influence in world affairs in the late nineteenth and early twentieth centuries, indeed, imperial statesmen saw it as one of their main duties to educate those fortunate enough to have been born in 'the empire on which the sun never sets' in the virtues of representative government. This was Britain's main beneficent legacy not only to Kipling's famous, though ironically intended, 'lesser breeds without the law', but also to its European neighbours. Britain had, after all, managed this subtle transformation without revolution; most of them had not. Historians of the early twentieth century rarely presented analyses as starkly or crudely as this, but important studies such as J. R. M. Butler's *The Passing of the Great Reform Bill* [48] and G. S. Veitch, *The Genesis of Parliamen-*

tary Reform [44] were untroubled by any reflection that the reforms they were explaining did not produce a political system which was an improvement on the one which it replaced. For Butler, in particular, the emphasis was on the success of the Whig leaders in revolution and thus in putting Britain on the progressive route to non-violent change (see Chapter 4).

Emphases have radically changed. First, history writing in a more cynical and less self-confident age no longer seeks to chart 'progress' from a lesser to a greater state, not least because late twentieth-century society has become much more ambivalent about what constitutes progress. Secondly, much more attention was given to continuities rather than change. Thus, for example, the 1832 Reform Act in no real sense gave 'power' to the middle classes. Britain was ruled, from Westminster at least, for two generations after it by a parliament dominated by landowners and a Cabinet whose members remained predominantly aristocratic. As Hanham put it in 1969, 'Everything possible was done [in 1832] to preserve the continuity of the great landed interests, which has dominated British politics since the seventeenth century' [10 *p. 12*]. Similarly, although the 1867 and 1868 Reform Acts produced working-class majorities in many urban constituencies, the same political parties – Liberal and Conservative – remained the contenders for political power, at least outside Ireland with its rising nationalist party. The Labour Representation Committee was not founded until 1900; it changed its name to 'the Labour Party' in 1906. Before the First World War, this supposedly 'working man's party' clung desperately to the coat tails of the Liberal party for political survival.

Thirdly, much more detailed work has been done at constituency level. Not surprisingly, this work has produced findings which do not point in the same direction. On the one hand, it is now clear that a significant number of parliamentary constituencies actually *lost* electors in the years after 1832. The new uniform borough franchise (see Chapter 4) excluded many working-class interests as pre-1832 voters died off. Thus, although big cities like Birmingham, Sheffield and Leeds gained direct representation and, with it, some of the largest constituencies in the country, others like Bristol, Liverpool and Hull had a considerably smaller proportion of adult males registered to vote in the early 1860s than they had in 1832 [13 *p. 57*]. In smaller boroughs, like Lancaster and Tamworth, the size of the electorate had dropped sharply by the 1850s.

It has also been argued that the nature of the political process underwent damaging change so far as the lower orders were concerned. Not only did many quasi-democratic constituencies disappear; those crucial elements of ritual and theatre associated with the hustings and very public assertions of political allegiance were dissipated when large numbers of polling stations were provided within convenient distance of the uniformly propertied electorate. A politicised 'crowd' of voters and non-voters alike could no longer congregate in the county town [71]. Elections, by accident or design, were sanitised.

POPULAR PARTICIPATION

Furthermore, historians have begun to question how important the vote actually *was* to participation in the political process. After a decade of political protest in the 1960s, many student leaders realised that storming the ramparts of university senates, and being recognised there as voting members, brought them no closer to actual power than before. In some respects, indeed, lucid and considered cases presented to a vice-chancellor in the form of a letter or memorandum might have more practical effect than heated speeches backed up by a few votes in the formal decision-making bodies. The parallel with national politics in the nineteenth century is closer than it might seem. As O'Gorman and Vernon have demonstrated [39; 71; 122; 128], the absence of votes was no bar to political participation. MPs needed to take account of a wide range of interests if they wished to remain on good terms with their constituencies. The possession of the vote and the possession of political influence were not necessarily the same thing. Both before and after 1832, it is more important to understand the political climate than to count changes in the number of voters. The suffragettes of the early twentieth century produced brilliant propaganda which highlighted how educated, intelligent and public-spirited women were denied the vote while brutish, drunken ignorant men could use it [108]. In reality, such campaigns were at least as much about the assertion of women's importance to a stable political system as they were to crosses on a ballot paper.

Growing concern with constituency politics was fortified by detailed studies of election statistics (psephology). Psephology made use of what historians quickly recognised was the vital raw material for such a study, the parliamentary 'poll books' which, in the years before the secret ballot was introduced in 1872, recorded who voted for whom. It was therefore possible to determine political allegiances both pre- and post-1832. This proved a vital new tool in determining how much the Great Reform Act changed voting habits and which social groups were likely to vote for which candidates and which parties [72]. Henry Pelling produced what he called a 'social geography' of elections after the passage of the Third Reform Act [87]. History thus fruitfully linked with both the quantitative and the qualitative techniques of the social sciences to develop analyses of parliamentary reform. One famously controversial study on the impact of 1832 (see Chapter 4) acknowledged its 'sociological premises' [54].

These political studies, related closely to social and occupational structures, link directly to two other important trends which have been developed during the last 40 years. 'History from below' flourished particularly in the 1960s and 1970s when many scholars became increasingly concerned with the importance of social structures. The quest to discover the origins both of the English 'working class' and, historiographically a little later, the British 'middle class' necessitated social analysis. The more perceptive of the historians of class recognised that growing political awareness was an integral part of the process. Class consciousness, after all, related to the exercise of power and the quest for power needed existing political structures to be changed [43; 55]. Thus, discussion of parliamentary reform became intertwined with debates about class and about the significance of a changing 'political culture' in nineteenth-century Britain.

HISTORIANS AND THE LINGUISTIC TURN

The other important intellectual development was the so-called 'linguistic turn'. This began to influence history-writing (not always for the better and, stylistically, very much for the worse) in the 1980s. Detailed study by historians of language as a transmitter of ideas, not necessarily yoked to social, economic or cultural assumptions about their significance, was inspired by radical new ideas in literary criticism conventionally described as 'post-structuralism'. The relevance, and even the validity, of this approach for historians steeped in an empirical tradition has excited much debate, both anguished and spiteful. Many have been reluctant to accept that language constructs its own reality, rather than being invented to meet economic, social or cultural needs. Certainly, extreme versions of post-structuralism, which argue that a text has no validity outside itself, undermine all forms of historical enquiry since they deny any notion of relative importance and suggest that change cannot be explained by prioritising (in other words self-consciously 'privileging' particular pieces of historical evidence). Even the links and connections which historians rely upon to test their hypotheses are considered invalid by many structuralists.

It is tempting to sweep post-structuralism aside as portentous, yet vacuous, intellectual baggage which has nothing of value for the historian and which will soon collapse under the weight of its own self-referential pretensions. Tempting, especially given the extraordinarily ugly and obscurantist language in which much post-structuralist writing is couched, but unwise. At the very least, the so-called 'linguistic turn' has caused historians to be more rigorous in testing their assumptions. Language can, indeed, be used to help shape ideas. Perhaps a fashion itself, it has nevertheless helped to debunk some earlier ones. A study of the language used by those democratic parliamentary reformers called Chartists, for example, conveys the obvious but still significant message that they wanted *political* change [60; 63]. Thus, the explanation for their movement is not to be reduced to a simple matter of hunger or economic privation. Nor is it inevitable that it was primarily a class-based movement.

Similarly, Dror Wahrman has stimulatingly and provocatively wrestled with that ubiquitous phrase 'the middle class'. He argues that it is more valid to see the term as a deliberate 'construct' rather than the result of inevitable social and economic development. Any reader still caught in that time warp within which generalisations like 'The 1832 Reform Act gave power to the middle classes' have currency will be shaken by observations such as 'it was not so much the rising "middle class" that was the crucial factor in bringing about the Reform Bill of 1832; rather, it was the Reform Bill of 1832 that was the crucial factor in cementing the invention of the ever-rising "middle class"' [45 *p. 18*). In his view, the 'middle class' was given a greater prominence by an aristocracy with power to preserve. It was less a reality than a politically convenient construct.

Thus have so many easy, progressive generalisations about reform been pulled apart or, in the jargon of the age, 'deconstructed'. Can Humpty Dumpty be put together again? It is the contention of this book that it can. Certainly, it is necessary to divest ourselves of some long-established, but unhelpful, generalisations. 'Progress' in political change is neither simple nor linear. The history of parliamentary reform is not the same thing as the history of democratisation. 'Democratisation' is anyway a highly problematic and contested concept. Non-voters are not necessarily politically excluded. No reform Act 'gives power' to any social group – at least not in any direct sense. Women were no more politically 'empowered' by the Reform Acts of 1918 and 1928 than were the middle ranks of society by that of 1832 [110]. It is more persuasive, if still not wholly convincing, to claim that nineteenth- and early twentieth-century reform Acts did more to confirm an established political order than to change one.

Historians have become more concerned with continuities. They play down the extent to which parliamentary reform changed the essentials. They may also be much more sceptical than they were about explanations which link changes in the franchise to changes in society contingent upon industrialisation. Much historical writing of the 1980s and 1990s has warned against 'economic reductionism' and indeed, any other form of reductionism [37]. This ungainly neologism merely states the obvious: complex phenomena are not to be explained by exclusive concentration on individual, or simpler, elements. However, historians' determination to try to see things 'in the round' has helped to clarify a number of issues relating to parliamentary reform. They are now more keenly aware that neither 'top-down' explanations, grounded in high politics at Westminster, nor 'bottom-up' ones, which concentrate on forms of extra-parliamentary pressure, are sufficient in themselves. The emphasis has shifted towards the need to understand that complex interplay of factors which created the active political culture of nineteenth- and early twentieth-century Britain. Changing methodological and interpretative fashions, therefore, have confirmed the central place of parliamentary reform within this culture. The subject needs robust and cogent explanation within this new framework.

2 PARLIAMENTARY REFORM AGITATION BEFORE 1832

ORIGINS TO 1789

Pressure to change both the composition of the House of Commons and the qualifications to vote long predates the first major parliamentary reform Act passed in 1832. The history of earlier reform movements will be followed in broad outline here; a number of useful studies exist to take the student deeper [7; 21; 27; 28; 29; 30; 49]. It was easy to criticise the unreformed political system. The number and distribution of parliamentary constituencies reflected medieval circumstances. By the later eighteenth century, they bore no relation to intrinsic economic and political importance. Cornwall sent 44 members to Parliament, one fewer than the whole of Scotland, which had been linked by political union to England in 1707. Rapidly industrialising Lancashire sent only 13. Although the great majority of English voters were to be found in county constituencies, the counties represented only 80 of England's 489 parliamentary seats. Each English county sent two MPs to parliament regardless of size or population.

Even greater anomalies existed over rights to vote in parliamentary elections. Every male owner of land worth at least 40 shillings (£2) a year in rental value could vote in a county constituency, though the exercise of voting rights could be a time-consuming and costly business because voting normally took place in the county towns. In the boroughs, however, voting rights varied widely from constituency to constituency. In a few well-populated places, such as Preston, Northampton, Coventry and Westminster, a majority of adult males could vote. Some constituencies before 1832, indeed, were close to being male democracies. Most, however, had very restricted voting rights. Students of parliamentary history are well aware of the names of the tiniest parliamentary boroughs, such as Old Sarum (outside Salisbury), Dunwich (on the Suffolk coast and already beginning to fall into the North Sea) or East and West Looe (Cornwall) where voters might be in single figures. In far more, voters did not top two hundred.

Many of these constituencies were in the control either of the Crown (through what was called 'court influence') or of an aristocratic patron (or 'borough monger' as he was often called). Most of Scotland's parliamentary seats at the end of the eighteenth century were controlled in the interest of the Crown and government by Henry Dundas, a senior minister of William Pitt the Younger.

In the smaller boroughs, actual elections were a rarity. Twenty-nine general elections were held in the years 1701–1831. The boroughs of Newton-le-Willows (Lancashire), Bere Alston (Devon) and West Looe (Cornwall) appear to have had no electoral contests whatever in this period [49]. Other boroughs held no more than two or three. In general, it was the larger boroughs, such as Liverpool, Maidstone, Lincoln and the City of London which saw the most frequent elections in the eighteenth and early nineteenth centuries.

Such a haphazard system had many critics, as we shall shortly see. It is important not to jump to the over-simple conclusion, however, that the combination of a highly restricted electorate and infrequent elections ensured a moribund political system. As Frank O'Gorman's work has demonstrated, non-voters were frequently politically aware and capable of formulating views and even policies which the political elite ignored at its peril [39; 122]. What was called 'maintaining the interest' in a constituency frequently involved engaging in lively debate with inhabitants. O'Gorman concludes that, although most constituencies were indeed controlled by great landowners or the crown, this control 'was exercised at great cost, with great care, with great difficulty, with much effort, and sometimes for no very great return' [39 p. 384]. The absence of an electoral contest was no guarantee of lack of political involvement. Agreements or accommodations between different interests were brokered between elections, or sometimes just before nominations closed: '... the results of elections were determined not so much by the electors as by the patron or patrons involving themselves in a complex and long-term dialogue with the community' [39 p. 386].

The revisionist picture which emerges, therefore, is of a vigorous and, at least to some extent, an inclusive political culture. Eighteenth-century politics during the so-called 'Whig Oligarchy' was not to be explained solely, or even primarily, by crude bribery and treating, with the aim of avoiding elections and ensuring that apathy, inertia and stasis ruled. Far too much attention had been paid by the school of historians inspired by Sir Lewis Namier to study the voting structure of constituencies without delving more deeply into the political and social interactions which were an essential element in political debate and control [38].

Although the unreformed system of politics was a good deal more flexible, responsive and, to a degree, representative than used to be thought, it was certainly not invulnerable to attack. Nevertheless, a sense of perspective is necessary. The structure of parliament was only one of a number of reformist targets in the eighteenth century and, at least until the 1790s, by no means the most important. Religious nonconformists and their supporters, for example, were much more concerned to be rid of discriminatory legislation against them, dating from the reign of Charles II. In the years 1787–89, particularly, it seemed for a time that the so-called Test and Corporations Acts would fall to a concerted campaign from dissenters and their allies in the Whig opposition to the government of the Younger Pitt. At much the same time, evangelical reformers were beginning to build up a head of steam against what they saw as the inhumanity and immorality of the slave trade. Earlier in the reign of George III (1760–1820), the campaigns of the populist politician John Wilkes highlighted the potential for conflict between the interests of government and those of elected MPs. Whether the clearly expressed will of the electorate could be overturned by parliament, which deemed Wilkes an ineligible MP despite successive re-elections for the county of Middlesex in 1768–69, became a major issue to stir popular opinion particularly in London [41]. The heightened tensions generated by Wilkes's campaigns over freedom of elections and reporting of parliamentary debates formed an important link to parliamentary reform agitation. In both, the existence of a strong 'oppositional' culture, embracing not only politicians out of office but also both the educated middle classes and an increasing number of skilled craftsmen, was important. Opposition might have been volatile in the 1760s and 1770s but it was becoming increasingly informed and sophisticated, nurtured by an increasingly popular provisional press, by a rash of pamphlets, squibs and cartoons, and by coffee-house society in which a range of opinions could be discussed [23].

Opposition politicians throughout the eighteenth century also became adept at using public opinion to attack governments which increased taxes, particularly when food prices were rising. Public opinion also polarised sharply over the conflict with the American colonies. Again, opposition politicians, led in the 1770s by the so-called Rockingham Whigs, attempted to mobilise public opinion against an ineffective government fighting an unpopular war against colonies whose cause many in Britain believed to be just. Central to the opposition campaign was the belief that the King was exerting undue influence. He was alleged to impose policies on his ministers and use patronage to achieve majorities in parliament which did not reflect the wishes of the people. This lay behind the famous motion which John Dunning presented to parliament in April 1780: 'that the influence of the crown has increased, is increasing and ought to be diminished'. With the war going very badly and the government in ever-increasing debt, enough loyal, though independent, MPs were persuaded to see Dunning's motion as an attack on the government of Lord North rather than on the person of the King [26; 32; 49]. Their votes contributed to a narrow victory (233–215) for this highly subversive resolution.

By the early 1780s, therefore, debate increasingly focused on how the power structure in Britain operated. It was but a small step from the opposition's so-called 'Economical Reform' programme (which aimed to reduce royal patronage) to support of parliamentary reform as a means of 'cleaning up' government. Wilkes declared himself a parliamentary reformer in a speech to the Commons in 1776 which asserted that 'The meanest mechanic, the poorest peasant and day-labourer has important rights concerning his personal liberty. ... Some share ... in the making of those laws which deeply interest them, and to which they are expected to pay obedience, should be reserved even to this inferior, but most useful, set of men' [49 *p. 67*]. Public opinion, which Wilkes so effectively roused on other constitutional issues, was at this stage indifferent. Parliamentary reform in the late 1770s was no 'bottom-up' movement which ordinary people forced on to the political agenda. Rather, it emerged as a weapon in the struggle for control within a social and political elite.

Certainly, the great majority of early parliamentary reformers already possessed the vote. One such was Major John Cartwright. He published a pamphlet, *Take Your Choice*, in 1776 in which he argued the democratic case, putting forward in the process all six points of the People's Charter of the late 1830s (see Chapter 5). After more than two years of Rockingham Whig pressure to reduce the power of the crown in British political affairs, Christopher Wyvill, a wealthy clergyman from a landed Yorkshire background, formed a 'Yorkshire Association' in December 1779 to co-ordinate pressure from outside Westminster in favour of economical reform [21; 49]. Three months later, the Association widened both its scope and its geographical focus, with the objective of presenting parliament with a number of petitions for parliamentary reform. In April 1780 a group of London radicals, led by Cartwright and John Jebb, formed the 'Society for Constitutional Information'. Although they excited considerable initial interest and stimulated the drafting of numerous pro-reform petitions, the new societies had little success. Even in London, the undisputed centre of radical opinion, the anti-Catholic Gordon Riots of 1780, which took parts of the capital out of the control of the authorities for almost a week, thoroughly alarmed propertied opinion. The riots dissuaded many from supporting any political initiative originating outside Westminster.

The reformers' cause revived as the American war tottered to its inglorious climax. Just before the fall of North's ministry in 1782, the young William Pitt proposed that parliament consider the reform issue since 'the people were loud for a *more equal representation*' [31]. He made more specific proposals in 1783, which included more members of parliament for the bigger towns and more populous counties but these were voted down by more than 150 votes. In accepting George III's invitation to form a government in December, however, Pitt also split the reformers. Charles James Fox, by now a confirmed parliamentary reformer, went into resentful opposition. He accused Pitt of treachery for co-operating with a monarch who, he believed, was hell-bent on subverting the constitution. Pitt's last attempt to reform parliament by offering the Commons a 'safe and temperate plan' took place in 1785. This was radical enough by the standards of the day. It proposed disfranchising the 36 smallest boroughs and transferring their 72 parliamentary seats to the larger counties and to London. The Commons rejected it by 248 votes to 174. Thus, even a prime minister with a secure majority for normal government business was not able to convince MPs of the necessity for reform. It was one of Pitt's few parliamentary defeats and he rapidly turned his attention to administrative and financial reform.

Before 1789, therefore, the parliamentary reform case had been widely aired but had not yet imprinted itself on the popular consciousness. Strong support for it could be drawn upon in London at times of more general unrest or agitation. Intellectuals, influenced by the European Enlightenment ideas of Voltaire and Rousseau, emphasised the irrationality and unrepresentativeness of the unreformed system. Some in the urban middle classes, particularly wealthier religious dissenters, were also convinced that reform was important both on grounds of rational improvement and also to slacken the grip of the landed interest on the levers of political power. Most of all, however, it was a useful stick with which to beat an unpopular government. Most of those who followed Wyvill and Cartwright in the early 1780s did so less because they were convinced by the merits of a specific reform scheme. Worked proposals were both rare and divisive. It is significant that, once Pitt had established himself in power and once national fortunes revived after the disastrous American war, pressure for parliamentary reform almost disappeared for the rest of the 1780s. In the years immediately before the French Revolution, extra-parliamentary pressure concentrated on religious, rather than political, reform [26; 39].

THE IMPACT OF THE FRENCH REVOLUTION

The French Revolution changed everything, although not immediately. In the short-term, most of the political elite welcomed it. The Revolution weakened Britain's natural enemy while also destroying Catholic absolutism. Whigs had been educated to believe that the great virtues of the Glorious Revolution had been the end of absolutism and the Protestant succession. 1789 was, therefore, widely seen as France's 1688. Three things quickly disabused Pitt's government of its faintly patronising reaction. Events in France from the second half of 1791 seemed to vindicate the prophecy of Edmund Burke in *Reflections on the Revolution in France* (1790) that the new forces unleashed by the revolution were dangerously uncontainable. Secondly, Britain was to be at war with revolutionary France from early 1793. It was, in consequence, necessary to raise troops at high speed and to instil a spirit of patriotic defiance in the British nation. Thirdly, this patriotic reaction was no foregone conclusion. By the end of 1791, it was clear that the French Revolution had been an energising force for many radicals. So quickly had things developed, indeed, that even some reformist Whigs were becoming alarmed. One such, George Tierney, wrote to another, Charles Grey, in October 1792 that 'The late events in France ... have made one party here desperate and the other drunk. Many are become wild Republicans who a few months ago were moderate Reformers' [45 *p. 31*]

Educated and enthused by Tom Paine's best-selling *Rights of Man* [*Doc. 1*], radicals established a number of political societies in Britain. They called for parliamentary reform and for changes in the system of government similar to those which had been recently effected in France. In particular, they were attracted to ideas about 'citizenship' and government based on consent rather than ancient authority. The ideas were not new but the social composition of the radical societies of the 1790s was. Many were organised and led by skilled working men. The best known was the London Corresponding Society, founded in 1792. Its first secretary was a shoemaker, Thomas Hardy, though he was assisted by a veteran middle-class radical John Horne Tooke. The first seems to have been the Sheffield Society for Constitutional Information, established at the end of 1791. This took its name from a London society dominated by the middle classes and dissenters, but most of its members appear to have been 'artisans' and 'mechanics'. These societies corresponded with each other and, far more worryingly for the authorities, with revolutionaries in France. A number of the societies established in Scotland in 1792–93 embraced French egalitarian symbolism. These were the first to feel the force of government response. Their leaders, the lawyer Thomas Muir and the English Unitarian minister, Thomas Fysshe Palmer, were convicted of sedition and transported [43].

Recent research has emphasised the weaknesses of the radical movements rather than seeing them as the harbingers of 'working-class' consciousness [7; 27]. As in the 1770s and 1780s, precise reformist objectives caused disagreement. Most artisan societies were genuinely democratic; others, and particularly those with a significant propertied influence, wanted to restrict the vote to householders. How parliamentary seats should be apportioned was also uncertain. Parts of Tom Paine's message were also divisive. Even convinced democrats were uneasy at a vigorous rationalism which embraced wholesale attacks on the clergy and, by implication, even religion itself. Many of the societies were hardly 'working-class' at all but reflected an alliance between the freethinking middle-ranks in society, including small tradesmen, and skilled workers. Unskilled and casual labourers seem to have been little affected by democratic or republican ideas. The numbers of members claimed by the new radical societies were often inflated by occasional attenders. In many cities, notably Birmingham and Manchester, radical societies were outgunned by conservative responses. 'Patriotism' was more potent than democracy as a rallying cry, particularly after the war began [5; 7; 27]. Mass support for parliamentary reform was not firmly rooted and tended to manifest itself only at times of economic crisis and high unemployment, such as the famine year of 1795.

The radical societies of the 1790s, however, did inundate parliament with petitions for parliamentary reform and the authorities were genuinely alarmed by such a popular upsurge of unrest. As early as May 1792, a proclamation was issued against 'seditious writings'. The main target was Tom Paine. 'We cannot see without indignation, the attempts which have been made to weaken in the minds of his majesty's subjects, sentiments of obedience ... and attachment to the form of government' [7 *p. 72*]. In 1794, Habeas Corpus was suspended, permitting the authorities to round up named suspects and to hold them indefinitely without trial. It was a tactic which would be periodically, and profitably, employed by governments well into the Chartist period [43; 49; 63]. At the end of the most politically disturbed year of all, 1795, two new Acts were passed against Seditious Meetings and Treasonable Practices.

Edward Thompson has argued that the Two Acts drove radicalism underground and helped to nurture a genuinely revolutionary tradition [43]. This is almost certainly an exaggeration. Some 'United Englishmen' and 'United Irishmen' did indeed plot. Some, like John Binns and Father James O'Coigly, tried to foment an English rebellion in 1798 to support the one which had broken out in Ireland. The Despard Conspiracy of 1803 was also a genuine attempt at a *coup d'état* based on plotting in England, Ireland and France. It claimed support both in London and industrial Lancashire [1; 43; 44]. Pitt's repressive policies against radicalism, however, if never overwhelmingly popular, were readily accepted not only among the propertied classes – those most directly threatened by revolutionary radicalism – but by many working people also. No popular majority for parliamentary reform existed during the French Wars of 1793–1815 [27].

If Pitt and his propagandists could successfully play the patriotic card, so far as parliamentary reform was concerned the prime minister had, Macbeth-like, 'scotched the snake, not killed it'. Current historiography might emphasise the relative weakness of the parliamentary reformers, argue that their organisations were easily cowed into submission and note that the reform campaign proceeded very much in fits and starts with long periods in which nothing much seemed to be happening. Parliamentary reform, however, never went away. In 1809, the aristocratic radical, Sir Francis Burdett, was elected MP for the constituency of Westminster. Westminster had a large electorate, including artisans and journeymen, and Burdett was able to tap into the constituency's long-standing tradition of radical support. His victory pushed parliamentary reform back on to the political agenda where it remained during the last years of the war, years which were characterised by the return of high food prices and unemployment. In 1810, Thomas Brand secured more than one hundred votes in a parliamentary motion to give the vote to all male householders. In 1812, Major John Cartwright was on the stump again in the Midlands and north-west using distress as a catalyst for further reform agitation. He urged workers to form Hampden Clubs – the name being taken from John Hampden, a notable opponent of Charles I's personal rule in the 1630s [25; 49].

PEACE AND THE REVIVAL OF REFORM, 1815-20

The return of peace was not accompanied by a return of economic prosperity. The reform question accordingly assumed greater prominence than ever. During the agitation which flared dangerously, if periodically, from 1815 to 1820, there was no war to deflect the thrust of the reformers' case. Some historians have considered this 'the heroic age of popular radicalism', a period in which radicals were able to establish a 'mass platform' in support of parliamentary reform [1; 22; 35; 43; 46]. This 'platform' was inadvertently strengthened by the government. In 1815, Lord Liverpool's administration passed a new Corn Law. It gave greater trade protection for farmers by, in effect, removing the threat of foreign competition. Liverpool argued that the Corn Law would encourage hard-pressed farmers to keep producing food [30 *p. 101*]. His many opponents preferred a more conspiratorial explanation. A parliament dominated by landowners would pass legislation protecting landowners. The consequence was high bread prices for the working classes. Meanwhile, the commercial and industrial classes could expect no protection from the legislature. The inflated prices to which the new Corn Law gave rise increased social tensions; they also presented parliamentary reformers with their strongest card yet.

These were also fruitful years for a radical press which carried the reformers' case with increasing confidence to all parts. It now found (unlike in the 1790s) a receptive audience in the northern industrial areas [3; 22; 29]. The skilled weaver, poet and journalist, Samuel Bamford, famously suggested – with only limited exaggeration – that 'the writings of William Cobbett suddenly became of great authority; they were read on nearly every cottage hearth in the manufacturing districts of South Lancashire, in those of Leicester, Derby and Nottingham; also in many of the Scottish manufacturing towns' [30 *p. 114*]. Cobbett's journalism was steeped in anti-aristocratic bile and hatred of a free trade system which he believed destroyed harmonious relations between rich and poor. Cobbett shed his earlier suspicion of Tom Paine's egalitarian doctrines and gave increasing space in the *Political Register* and *Twopenny Trash* to the necessity of parliamentary reform. So did Thomas Wooler's *Black Dwarf*, published from 1817 to 1824, and William Sherwin's *Weekly Political Register* (1817–19) and *Manchester Observer* (1818–21). Radical journalism, published at a deliberately low price to catch the mass audience, increasingly advocated universal manhood suffrage as the preferred outcome of parliamentary reform rather than a household or any other form of more limited suffrage.

Alongside radical journalism went reform petitions organised by Hampden and 'Union' Clubs and, especially, mass political meetings. These were summoned by radical leaders in order to pass democratic resolutions and to remind the people that their miseries were caused by government corruption and high taxes. Three major meetings were held in Spa Fields, London, in 1816–17. One precipitated a riot and the threat of disorder at this time. Much the most famous meeting, that held to hear the Wiltshire farmer Henry 'Orator' Hunt preaching reform in St Peter's Fields, Manchester, in August 1819, did not produce riot but its forcible break-up by army cavalry coming to the aid of a panicky Manchester Yeomanry involved 11 deaths [22]. This event, rapidly christened 'Peterloo', a mocking reference to the Battle of Waterloo, gave the radical cause its first innocent martyrs. The government, which fiercely criticised the actions of the yeomanry in private, found it much more difficult to suggest that it adequately represented public opinion after Peterloo.

The years 1815–20 were crucial to the cause of parliamentary reform. Support grew markedly; by 1820 parliamentary reform could be described as a genuinely national crusade. The established method of bringing grievances to the attention of the legislature – petitions to parliament – went into overdrive. In the disturbed year 1817, more than 700 petitions were presented. Most either drew attention to economic woes, or called for reform of government, or both. More than 60 per cent came from the industrialising Midlands and North of England, providing powerful evidence of the vigour of reformist political culture in urban Britain [5 *p. 76*]. We should beware of representing these years as a kind of triumphal reformist progress, however. Relations between genuine democrats, like Hunt and Wooler, and the more moderate reformers were frequently strained. When reformers met together, they argued. The first assembly of the reform spokesmen, held at the Crown and Anchor Tavern in London in January 1817, revealed fundamental splits between those who favoured a householder and a full manhood suffrage. Hunt and Cobbett squabbled; Sir Francis Burdett stayed away [49 *p. 168*].

Popular support for reform was also directly proportional to the extent of economic distress. In 1816–17, for example, Liverpool's government responded to growing support for radicalism with the same clamp down on political liberties which the Younger Pitt had pioneered in the early 1790s. In 1819, Liverpool and Sidmouth responded to renewed disaffection after Peterloo by passing their famous 'Six Acts', more extensive in scope than Pitt's Two Acts in 1795. In late 1817 and during 1818, however, the situation had been far less disturbed during a temporary economic recovery. Despite its evident alarm at the mass meetings and myriad other signs of popular disaffection, therefore, the government could still claim, first, that pressure for parliamentary reform was largely temporary 'hunger politics' and, secondly, that repressive measures would be sufficient to frighten the majority into submission. The government, well-provided with both spies and *agents provocateurs*, never lost control of events in this period [8; 43]. It could also reflect that increasingly influential urban and commercial propertied opinion, however much it was with government policy, feared disorder and threats of revolution from below a sight more than it hated aristocratic rule. The reformers' case was far from won.

PART TWO: THE 'GREAT' REFORM ACT OF 1832

3 CAUSES: EXTERNAL PRESSURE OR INTERNAL COLLAPSE?

THE DOWNFALL OF TORYISM

The previous chapter explained why parliamentary reform was firmly on the political agenda by the 1820s. Inevitably, the Reform Act of 1832 had long-term causes. This chapter is concerned with short-term causes. It aims to explain not so much why the Reform Act was passed but why it was passed *in 1832*. In particular it deals with the increasingly controversial question: 'Was reform passed primarily because of growing extra-parliamentary pressure, or did it result from decisive short-term changes within Westminster itself?'

> Do not you think that the tone of England ... is more liberal – to use an odious but intelligible phrase – than the policy of the government? ... It seems to me a curious crisis – when public opinion never had such influence on public measures, and yet never was so dissatisfied with the share it possessed. It is growing too large for the channels it is accustomed to run through ... Can we resist – I mean not next session or the session after that – but can we resist for seven years reform in Parliament?

The extract from a famous letter written in March 1820 by one strong anti-reformer, the young Sir Robert Peel, to another, the Tory journalist and politician John Wilson Croker, helped persuade the historian John Cannon that, in the early 1820s, the parliamentary reform question 'changes from a crusade to become an accepted creed' [49 *pp. 182–3*]. During the 1820s, he argues, anti-reformers were forced 'stage by stage ... on to the defensive'. Put another way, the argument is that parliamentary reform ceased to be the preserve of a group of extreme radicals and intellectuals and entered a political mainstream still overwhelmingly dominated by landowners. Increasingly, the question became not *whether* reform would come, but *when*.

This view suggests an evolutionary interpretation. Pressure had been building at least since the early 1790s. It had reached such a pitch by the early 1820s, converting such a wide cross-section of society outside Westminster, that even anti-reformers were becoming convinced that reform could not be held back indefinitely. As Cannon puts it: 'In 1820 and 1821 began that tiny shift of pebbles that anticipates the avalanche, as, one by one, members began to announce their conversion to reform' [49 *p. 183*]. In 1822, the leading Whig politician Lord John Russell introduced a bill to take away one of the two parliamentary seats held by the hundred smallest boroughs and redistribute them to the counties and large towns with no separate representation [*Doc. 4*] . It was defeated but received more votes than any reform bill since Pitt's in 1785. The tide seemed to be turning. Grey, the Whig leader, had believed before 1820 that he would not see reform in his lifetime. From the early 1820s he became more optimistic. When anti-reformers felt that it was more dangerous to deny reform than to accede to it, then it became inevitable. There is, however, a very different interpretation of why reform came about when it did.

This alternative interpretation is sceptical about the ability of parliamentary reformers outside Westminster to sustain pressure at levels sufficient to frighten governments into action against their better judgement. From 1783 to 1830, British government was dominated by Pittites and Tories [3; 7; 24]. From the early 1790s, they were implacably opposed to parliamentary reform since they believed that concessions risked leaving Britain open to a French-style revolution. As Harling puts it, 'the vast majority of Tories were adamantly opposed to any significant extension of political rights; they assumed that substantial parliamentary reform would subvert the political hierarchy and bring about a social revolution' [33 *p. 151*].

The reform cause, it is true, had built up impressively from the early 1770s. However, it had only seemed threatening when linked to adverse economic factors, usually high prices, high levels of unemployment or both. Governments had been able to take the heat out of the situation by passing repressive legislation, locking up radical leaders and generally battening down the hatches of liberty until the economy began to boom again. Economic recovery invariably ebbed the tide of parliamentary reform. Peel's colleagues *were* able to resist a reform in parliament for more than seven years because most of those years were prosperous. Reformers would still present petitions [*Doc. 5*]. Leaders like Cobbett, Hunt, Carlile and Wade still addressed their meetings and penned their pro-reform articles in which 'Old Corruption' was lambasted as roundly as ever [*Docs 2 and 3*]. Outwardly, at least, they remained supremely confident of success but they could claim no 'mass platform' in the mid-1820s. The few attempts to introduce parliamentary reform motions (see Chapter 2 and Chronology) in the Commons were easily seen off – usually by almost insultingly large majorities. While the government was in the hands of anti-reformers, therefore, there was no prospect that it would crumble in the face of extra-parliamentary hostility.

This analysis sees parliamentary reform not as a triumph for extra-parliamentary radicalism but as the result of the collapse of the Tory party in the years 1827–30. The severe stroke which Lord Liverpool suffered in February 1827 ushered in three years of extreme instability within the Tory party [31; 36; 51]. For several years, it had struggled to contain divisions over whether to give more concessions to Roman Catholics [42]. Liverpool had been an emollient figure and more politically shrewd than is usually recognised. His successors polarised opinions within the Tory party. Canning's prime ministership was brief; he died in August 1827. However, his reputation as a leading 'liberal' on the Catholic question was already causing severe strains. His government was more accurately described as a moderate Tory/Whig coalition than a purely Tory one. Lord Goderich, who succeeded him, had been an efficient and successful minister. He now revealed himself as a hopeless leader. He was replaced by the Duke of Wellington in January 1828. Wellington initially attempted to reunite the party but his basically authoritarian nature and his aversion to reform soon alienated Canningite 'liberal Tories', provoking the most senior of them into withdrawing from his government in May 1828. Then the major crisis in Ireland which led Wellington and Peel to concede Roman Catholic Emancipation in 1829 utterly destroyed whatever fragile unity remained in the party since the so-called 'Ultra' Tories felt betrayed by ministers they believed to be as 'anti-Catholic' as themselves. It was thus a divided and demoralised Tory party which had to grapple with the return of economic distress and, with it, the resurgence of reform agitation in late 1829 and early 1830.

Anti-reforming Toryism had emerged in the shadow of the French Revolution at the end of the eighteenth century, cushioned by the long and usually stable ministries first of Pitt and then of Liverpool. It dominated a generation. Although signs of disunity, particularly over religious questions, were growing during the 1820s, the speed and completeness of Tory collapse came as a profound shock. For one historian [24], the years 1828–32 represented the end of the *Ancien Régime*. The extreme conservatism of Clark's overall interpretation has not found much favour with historians, but his recognition that this period was decisive has been more widely accepted. Parliamentary reform came about more because of dramatic, and sudden, changes in the balance of power at Westminster rather than because of the heroic efforts of extra-parliamentary radicals.

THE REFORM CRISIS, 1829-32

Contending explanations for the passage of a parliamentary reform Act in 1832, therefore, can be broadly divided into long-term, extra-parliamenary and short-term, parliamentary ones. The specific events of 1829-32, however, can be used to support either interpretation. On the one hand, the return of 'hunger politics' brought crowds back on to the streets and led to a further increase in the petitioning campaign aimed at getting government to redress genuine grievances. Journalists and veteran radicals were on the scene to mount a pro-reform campaign of greater intensity, and probably greater threat, than ever before. Looked at in this light, the extra-parliamentary agitation of 1829-32 was the natural climax of a half-century of focused, if sporadic, agitation.

On the other hand, it was of first importance that this agitation was focused on a Tory government weaker in the House of Commons than any since 1794. The anti-reform Tory coalition had been shattered by the middle of 1830. Many, even of Wellington's nominal supporters, were anxious to see his government come to an end. On this interpretation, parliamentary reform came about in 1832 because a Whig government, under the veteran parliamentary reformer, Earl Grey, had come into office in November 1830, not because of coercion from outside. A Whig government ruled Britain because of desperate Tory divisions, not because of popular opinion. There is no obvious reason to suppose that extra-parliamentary agitation would have been more successful in coercing an anti-reform government in 1830-32 than it had been in 1815-20 or during the 1790s. In the words of Peter Jupp, 'Britain's political culture retained [into the 1830s] a cohesiveness during a period of rapid change in both its internal and external circumstances – a cohesiveness which radical activity such as that in the immediate postwar years challenged, but did not destroy' [36 *p. 446*].

The economic disturbances of 1829-31 were undoubtedly severe. Harvests were deficient in both 1828 and 1829 and food prices rose dramatically. More than 200 petitions were sent to parliament from the rural areas in February–March 1830 alone, most of them calling for reductions in taxation. In response, Wellington's government reduced duties on malt, beer and leather. When conditions failed to improve, the authorities faced their most direct challenge through the so-called 'Swing Riots' which broke out first in August 1830 and continued to disturb much of southern and eastern England over the next 18 months

[34]. The normal pattern included burning hay ricks and attacks on authority figures accused of not fulfilling their traditional duties. These included Church of England clergymen who levied full tithes at a time of agricultural depression and poor law overseers who exercised their responsibilities harshly or unfeelingly. The Swing Riots were community protests which, although only rarely concerned with parliamentary reform, forcibly indicated that social cohesion in the countryside had broken down. They had an important political impact on a parliament of landowners.

Depression also struck in the urban areas, provoking the by now predictable response. Radicals were able to get distressed workers on to the streets protesting about Old Corruption and calling for reform. William Cobbett, for example, delivered a series of pro-reform lectures in Manchester in January 1830 before moving across the Pennines to pass on the same message in Halifax, Huddersfield and Leeds. In the industrial textile districts of Lancashire and Yorkshire, the revived reform campaign followed hard upon strikes in 1828–29 and other labour protests against wage cutting during the trade depression. In London, Henry Hunt launched a new Radical Reform Association in September 1829 [21; 22]. The vigour of the radical press returned and circulations began once again to soar. Henry Hetherington's *Poor Man's Guardian* in London and John Doherty's *Voice of the People* in Manchester were only two of the journals which publicised the reformist case on behalf of a predominantly working-class readership. Pro-reform placards also began to festoon the larger towns.

In 1830–31, however, perhaps the more significant development was the extent of support among the middle classes for reform. Whereas during the post-war period, many small property owners seemed still to fear a French-style revolution, by 1830 anti-aristocratic (and particularly anti-Tory) sentiments were more prominent. Distrust of government economic policy undoubtedly played an important role. Not only did the famous Corn Laws discriminate in favour of landowners, but a landowners' parliament proved unresponsive to demands from the great commercial and industrial centres for relief from currency restrictions. Many of the greatest industrial towns, Birmingham, Leeds and Sheffield, had no direct representation in parliament. MPs also had far less direct knowledge of conditions in the industrial areas than they did of the countryside and tended to respond less sympathetically to urban petitions for relief. To many in the middle classes, therefore, an increased urban electorate and a larger number of members of parliament representing the north of England and the Midlands seemed to be the answer.

The Birmingham Political Union was founded in the last days of 1829 to press just this case. The BPU was the brainchild of Thomas Attwood, a banker who would become Birmingham's first MP in 1832. For Attwood, removing credit restrictions and issuing more paper money – the so-called 'Brummagem remedy' – were more important to Britain's future prosperity than the passage of reform, but he now believed that the one had become contingent on the other. He also had the political acumen to realise that a carefully integrated campaign which united middle and working classes would put greater pressure on government than ever before. The number of Political Unions spread rapidly in the early months of 1830. While the degree of harmony which obtained between democrats like Hunt and Hetherington and middle-class reformers like Attwood can easily be exaggerated, there is no doubt that the Political Unions represented a new, and more potent, reformist force. The middle classes provided money, organisation and – crucially – respectability to the reform campaign.

Their work was especially valuable to Whig reformers. Parliamentary reform and Whiggery were by no means synonymous terms. Even Earl Grey had frequently expressed doubts during his long career about the political wisdom of embracing reform since it was such a divisive issue [50; 58]. Many Whigs, and especially the Liberal Tories who joined him in coalition in 1830, were much less enthusiastic. Melbourne and Palmerston, to name only two future prime ministers, were decidedly lukewarm about the whole idea. The success of the Political Unions during 1830 convinced the doubters that a Whig government could hardly avoid reform. Representations of an increasingly powerful and enlightened middle class as an improving force united in support of reform entered the language of pro-Whig politicians. As early as 1821, John Lambton, Grey's son-in-law and later first Earl of Durham, was asserting that 'the *middle classes* of the population, the *very sinews* of the population, are eager and desirous of Reform' [25; 30; 45]. In 1831, John Sinclair, reflecting on the current clamour for reform, was offering the doubters another important argument. The middle-classes could be trusted to behave wisely but, left without pro-reform leadership from Westminster, they might remain dangerous allied to the demagogues and democrats who were exciting the passions of the working classes. This was an alliance at all costs to be broken: 'The elective franchise ought only to be intrusted to those who would exercise it with most wisdom and independence, and as wisdom and independence certainly prevail more in the middling ranks than in the whole mass of the people, the elective franchise should accordingly be principally enjoyed by them' [45 *pp. 254, 298*].

In the autumn of 1831, Grey told the King's private secretary that 'It is undeniable ... that the middle classes ... are activated by an intense and almost unanimous feeling in favour of the measure of reform' [7 *p. 220*].

The pro-reform tide, then, was flowing strongly by the middle of 1830. As so often in such circumstances, luck, as well as judgement, deserted the Tories. George IV, as hostile to reform as his prime minister, died in June. His successor, William IV, was far less politically experienced and, probably because he had not reflected on the subject over-much, was not so antagonistic. More important for Wellington, however, George's death necessitated a general election. This did not dramatically weaken the Tories' position. At most, they suffered a loss of 30 seats or so. They kept what would normally have been a workable majority in the Commons while a number of well-known pro-reform Whigs actually lost their seats. However, in the larger constituencies where public opinion counted for most, the Tories suffered significant defeats. The Home Secretary's brother, Jonathan Peel, was defeated in Norwich, for example [30 *pp. 118–19*]. By the autumn of 1830, Wellington was very much on the defensive and after a disastrously misjudged attempt to pretend that the unreformed parliament 'possessed the full and entire confidence of the country' [30 *p. 121*] support ebbed alarmingly. He left office in November to be replaced by a coalition government of Whigs and 'liberal Tory' defectors from the Duke of Wellington [*Doc. 6*]. It was headed by Earl Grey, the first prime minister with a parliamentary reform agenda since the Younger Pitt in 1785.

Events moved very rapidly from the end of 1830. The Whigs' reform bill, revealed in March 1831, may seem modest since it promised no secret ballot and a uniform voting qualification in the boroughs designed expressly to ensure that very few of the new voters would be working men (Appendix I). This was not how it seemed to MPs at Westminster. They counted the number of seats to be disfranchised and transferred with alarm, if not panic. The far-from-alarmist political commentator Charles Greville called it a 'sweeping measure indeed'. The bill was given a second reading by a majority of just one vote (302–301) in an unprecedentedly full House of Commons. When, as was inevitable, it began to be hacked to pieces in the detailed committee work, Grey asked for, and received, a dissolution from the King. The general election of 1831, a virtual plebiscite on reform, produced just the unequivocal result the Whig reformers wanted. Only six MPs who had voted against reform in the Commons were returned to the new parliament and the pro-reformers had a majority over their opponents of nearly 140.

Reform, therefore, was won in the Commons but not in the Lords. In a state of high public excitement, the Lords' rejection of the reform bill in October 1831 precipitated widespread rioting; riots debilitated towns as large as Nottingham and Bristol [47; 49]. The Whigs could use this to strengthen their message that reform was now imperative to guard against revolution. Grey, addressing the Lords the following month, tried hard to persuade rootedly antagonistic peers that his strategy was far more preferable to the alternative:

> If any persons suppose that this Reform will lead to ulterior measures, they are mistaken; for there is no one more decided against annual parliaments, universal suffrage, and the ballot, than I am. My object is not to favour, but to put an end to such hopes and projects. [7 *p. 223*]

Arguments like these eventually persuaded a majority of peers to vote against their instincts. The reform crisis was not over, however, until Grey resigned in May 1832, after failing immediately to persuade the King to create 50 new peers and so drive a reform majority through the upper house. Wellington tried, and failed, to form a new Tory government. His efforts were accompanied by the events of the so called 'Days of May': a fusilade of hostile petitioning, street demonstrations and reformist threats to destroy government finance by withdrawing savings from banks: 'to stop the Duke, go for gold' [47]. Only when Wellington told the King that he was unable to form a government did the activity abate. The Lords capitulated and voted through a measure most of them loathed. The so-called 'Great' Reform Act for England and Wales received the royal assent on 7 June 1832 (see p. 129).

Though the Whigs might not have come into office at all had it not been for the implosion of Toryism in 1827–30, it is difficult to see how they would have convinced the doubters in their own party, let alone hostile peers, to pass a reform bill had it not been for the unprecedentedly powerful, and co-ordinated, support for reform outside Westminster. Extra-parliamentary reformers were deeply divided about *how much* reform there should be but divisions on crucial details were submerged by the united feeling that the old system had to go. For their part, the Whigs' purpose in passing reform was perfectly clear. It was not to advance the cause of radical reform and democracy but to check it by creating a stable 'propertied alliance' between the landowning and the middle classes. Their objective was to conserve. The next chapter examines in what ways, and how far, they succeeded.

4 CONSEQUENCES: CHANGE OR CONTINUITY?

CONTINUITY AND REGRESSION

Did the Reform Act do more to change, or to consolidate, the existing political system? A recent study of the late 1820s and early 1830s suggests that the reform crisis can be seen as 'the culmination of an accelerating process of change within the political system, and offered the parliamentary elite an opportunity to make Parliament and the public more manageable' [*36 p. 448*]. Another historian, who has rescued the unreformed political system from the charge that it was corrupt and moribund, concluded that reform left the fundamentals unchanged: 'After all, the Reform Bill was the brainchild of men who not only knew the unreformed electoral system but who owed their careers in some measure to its existence. ... One electoral system disappeared and gave way to one remarkably like itself. The men, the institutions, the values and the practices are remarkably similar each side of 1832' [*39 p. 392*]. The Whigs thus seized an opportunity to amend the old order in their favour. They had no intention of reducing the political influence of the existing governing classes.

The 'continuity' thesis is superficially attractive. It is easy to list what the so-called 'Great' Reform Act did *not* change: no shorter parliaments; no secret ballot; no constituencies of the same size; no payment of MPs who anyway still needed a hefty property qualification before they could take their seats; certainly no manhood suffrage. The democratic agenda, so forcefully urged in 1830–32, had to be carried over unamended into the famous six points of the Chartist petition in 1838. Digging deeper into the structure of politics, rather than scratching its representational surface, the continuity picture still seems sharply in focus. The same parties – Whig and Tory – vied for supremacy, though they gradually changed their official names to 'Liberal' and 'Conservative'. A significant number of parliamentary seats remained effectively in the control of powerful aristocratic proprietors. Norman Gash estimated that upwards of 70 seats were in this position [53].

Interestingly, William Gladstone, perhaps the most famous political figure of the nineteenth century, made his entrance into the House of Commons in December 1832, aged 23, at the first general election held under the new rules. He represented Newark, in Nottinghamshire, and he did so as a Tory. His election was, in effect, controlled by the Duke of Newcastle, who owned much of the land in the town, and who had admired the staunch anti-reform stand the young Gladstone had taken as President of the Oxford Union. Support was also forthcoming from Lord Winchilsea. His agent told Gladstone that any 'erroneous notions' the peer's tenants might have as to the right way to vote would be duly 'corrected' [68 *pp. 40–1*]. Gladstone assured Newcastle of his belief in the 'virtues of an ancient aristocracy, than which the world never saw one more powerful or more pure'. He was duly returned top of the poll. The dominant political figure of the nineteenth century, who would symbolise progressive reform for many Liberal supporters in the second half of the nineteenth century, entered parliament in much the same way as his predecessors, Charles James Fox, William Pitt the Younger and Robert Peel: as a promising young man nominated by an influential borough patron on grounds of political loyalty first and ability second.

Thus, the 1832 Reform Act did not do away with what its defenders tended to call 'influence' at elections and its detractors called 'corruption'. Voters remained open to various forms of persuasion. At the 1832 election for the large borough of Preston, which had had a substantial working-class electorate, the veteran radical Henry Hunt, who had represented the town since 1830, was soundly defeated by a Whig–Tory coalition formed by two powerful local landowning families, the Stanleys and the Fleetwoods. Hunt retained the support of most radical working men and explained to them his view that 'Money, bribery, treating, intimidation, and hired bludgeon-men have prevailed and the working classes of Preston must remain in the hands of the Whig and Tory factions, till they have the protection of the ballot' [22 *p. 268*].

Hunt may have been looking for an excuse, of course, and he did at least stand as candidate in an election in which more than 5,300 men voted. Well-organised propertied opinion, in an election where there was no need to split the 'respectable' vote on party lines, proved more potent than working-class radicalism. The 1832 election was unusual in the number of constituencies in which a poll took place. Of the 254 constituencies, 188 (74 per cent) experienced an election. This was far higher than elections held before the Reform Act, when the proportion was never higher than 40 per cent. It is worth noting that enthusiasm for electoral contests began to wane. By 1847, only 47 per cent of seats had contests, although the proportion between the first two reform Acts was usually 60 per cent [7 *p. 405*].

In terms of direct representation at Westminster, the Reform Act was no 'middle-class triumph'. The Whigs intended that the lower middle classes would have the vote in 1832 – most of the wealthier middle classes could vote already – not that middle-class representation in the House of Commons would dramatically increase. Some manufacturers and other commercial figures found their way into a reformed parliament easily enough. The Commons had to endure the ex-draper and corrupt railway magnate George Hudson as Conservative MP for Sunderland, for example, from 1845 until his defeat in the election of 1859. The novelist and civil servant Anthony Trollope invented 'Mr Bott' as the stereotype of the blunt and unsophisticated industrial MP in his political novels of the 1850s and 1860s. Bott, complete with frightful northern accent, became the predictable butt of snobbish jokes from Plantagenet Palliser's aristocratic political friends. Trollope's stereotype was not wrong; nor was it typical. Industrial middle-class MPs there certainly were between 1832 and 1867 but it is striking how little the social composition of parliament changed. Landowners continued to provide between 70 and 80 per cent of the membership of the House of Commons. Sons and other near relatives of the aristocracy – 267 of the 658 MPs in the parliament of 1847 were categorised thus – remained a much more substantial category than did industrialists, few of whom could afford the time away from managing their businesses, even if they were attracted by the social and political excitements of London, which few seem to have been, at least on a semi-permanent basis.

We should also remember that the House of Commons had never been short of 'middle-class' MPs anyway. If not numerically dominant, many lawyers, journalists and other professions had long been making some of the liveliest, and most cerebral, contributions to debates there. Aristocratic power groups had long recognised the need to have articulate and creative supporters from the educated elite. Long before he alerted MPs to the dangers of the French Revolution and thus helped lay the foundations for a new Tory party, for example, the Dublin lawyer Edmund Burke had been a vital member of the Rockingham Whig circle. One of Burke's most effective antagonists in the 1790s, James Mackintosh, was a professor of law and later an influential contributor to the Whig *Edinburgh Review*. He was successively MP for Nairnshire, in northern Scotland and Knaresborough in Yorkshire. In the Commons he supported Catholic emancipation and moderate parliamentary reform. During the crisis of 1830–32, Thomas Babington Macaulay, son of a leading anti-slavery campaigner and grandson of a Scottish minister, was perhaps the most articulate and effective Whig spokesman for the case to 'reform in order to preserve' [47]. As he told the Commons in March 1831: 'the right of suffrage should depend upon a pecuniary qualification. ... I oppose universal suffrage because I think it would produce a destructive revolution. I support this measure, because I am sure that it is our best security against a revolution' [31; 47; 48].

The so-called Chandos Amendment, which gave votes to the more substantial tenant farmers, increased the county electorate by about 130,000. This development, however, not only confirmed but even extended, the electoral power of the aristocracy. The evidence that tenant farmers usually, though not invariably, voted according to the expressed preferences of their landowner is compelling. At the election for South Lincolnshire in 1841, indeed, in 32 of the 44 parishes owned by one man, all the tenants voted for that landowner's preferred candidate [69 p. 36].

It is possible to argue that the Reform Act, so far from 'improving' the political system, actually put it into reverse. Existing voters after 1832 kept their voting rights in their lifetimes. Significant numbers of artisans and others were thus entitled to register for the vote under the new rules. They could not, of course, pass on this privilege to their heirs and successors. The consequences are startling. The number of men entitled to vote after 1832 increased by perhaps 50 per cent [6; 128]. In many of the largest pre-1832 constituencies, by contrast, voting numbers steadily fell after 1832. Preston's 5,300 voters in 1832 had been reduced to fewer than 2,000 by 1857. In Northampton, the 2,372 voters of 1832 had dwindled to about 1,500 in 1857. Lancaster's electorate declined similarly, from 2,500 in 1832 to 1,400 in 1852. Expressed as proportions of adult males entitled to vote, the figures for many of the quasi-'democratic' constituencies of pre-reform England are even more stark. In Preston in 1832, 88 per cent of males were entitled to vote; this had plummeted to 11.6 per cent by 1851. The decline over the same period in Gloucester was from 51 per cent to 17.9 per cent and in Northampton from 64.9 to 24 per cent and in George Hudson's Sunderland from 43 to 11 per cent [13 p. 57]. In newly enfranchised boroughs, it is true, the trend was the other way; Birmingham and Leeds showed a substantial increase in males eligible to vote between 1832 and 1852. Still, it is possible to understand why those historians who are most persuaded of the political vitality of England before 1832 should see the Reform Act as reactionary. Few, however, would go as far as James Vernon's judgement of the period 1815–67: 'English politics became progressively less democratic during this period as political subjectivities and the public political sphere were defined in increasingly restrictive and exclusive fashions' [71 *pp. 8–9*].

Contemporary radical commentators were not slow to argue that 1832 had cheated the working classes. The editor of *Poor Man's Guardian*, Henry Hetherington, was scathing [*Doc. 7*] in his condemnation of an Act designed to preserve as much of the old order as possible. A few years later, Karl Marx argued that the Bill had nothing to do with representation and much with narrow political advantage 'by a series of the most extraordinary tricks, frauds and juggles ... calculated not for increasing middle-class influence, but for the exclusion of Tory and the promotion of Whig patronage' [*56 p. 24*].

CHANGE AND THE CULTURE OF REFORM

After such an extended exposition of the 'continuity' thesis, readers might be surprised to learn that opponents of reform tended to regard the changes brought about in 1832 as revolutionary, not to say apocalyptic. But they did. Here is the Duke of Wellington, writing to a fellow peer, the Duke of Buckingham, three weeks after the Reform Act received the royal assent:

> It is not in my power to prevent the consequence of the mischief which has been done. The Government of England is destroyed. A parliament will be returned, by means of which no set of men will be able to conduct the administration of affairs, and to protect the lives and properties of the King's subjects.

The Tory journalist and MP John Wilson Croker, who had represented six constituencies (most of them small boroughs) in a parliamentary career which stretched back to 1807, refused to stand for the reformed parliament: 'The reform Bill is a stepping stone in England to a republic. The Bill once passed, goodnight to the monarchy and the Lords and the Church.' It is easy to poke fun at prophecies which proved disastrously wide of the mark. Nevertheless, the 'continuity' thesis has been pushed too far. The Reform Act *did* change things, and with adverse long-term consequences for the landed interest, albeit neither to the degree nor at the speed which Wellington and Croker gloomily foretold.

Nineteenth- and early twentieth-century interpretations did, of course, provide easy targets for what might be termed a 'conservative' historiographical reaction. W. N. Molesworth's *History of the Reform Bill of 1832*, published in 1865 as pressure for a further instalment was building up, for example, should be taken with several pinches of salt. In support of his belief that the Act did indeed deserve the title 'Great', he asserted that it should 'be regarded by every Englishman with feelings of unmixed pride and satisfaction'. While the lower orders 'greatly exaggerated the effects which that measure would produce, and overlooked many causes of distress which it would not remove, but still they were right in their belief that it would tend to ameliorate their condition, as the event has abundantly proved' [56 p. 25]. The most scholarly and detailed assessment to be published before the First World War took the progressive line even further. J. R. M. Butler argued that 1832 placed 'the feet of the nation ... in the direction of democracy' [48 p. vii]. This is reading history backwards, in the knowledge of what came after.

A reaction was inevitable. As early as 1915, Charles Seymour was noting that 'The immediate political effects of the Reform Act ... proved less striking than many had anticipated' [20 pp. 102–3]. Norman Gash is perhaps the most distinguished of the many more recent historians who have argued that the Reform Act had limited significance, at least in the short term: 'it would be wrong to assume that the political scene in the succeeding generation differed essentially from that of the preceding one' [52 p. x]. Yet this seems to me to miss the point. It is not so much in the number of voters and the rearrangement of seats that the true measure of the Reform Act is to be seen.

Even here, though, it is important to recognise unconscious Anglocentrism. Many who criticise the conservatism of parliamentary reform have an unremittingly English perspective. The numerical changes in Scotland and Ireland, each of which had its own Reform Act, were far greater [12; 62; 124]. Scotland's increased the number of voters much more dramatically than did its English equivalent (see p. 130). About 4,000 voters before 1832 became 65,000 afterwards: approximately one in eight of the adult male population. Not surprisingly, this introduced a measure of representative politics in the process, both in the new parliamentary boroughs of Greenock and Paisley and also in the largest cities like Glasgow and Dundee. No longer could Scotland be characterised almost as one vast rotten borough, uncritically supportive of the court and any court-supported government of the day, the usual situation since the political Union of 1707. As late as 1826 an entire general election could pass by without one Scottish seat being contested. One of the driving forces behind the Scottish

Act, Henry Cockburn, claimed that it gave Scotland 'a political constitution for the first time' [14 p. 391], though later commentators have emphasised its many weaknesses [125]. In particular, the county seats remained overwhelmingly in the control of substantial landowners, who mostly supported Tory candidates [86 p. 87]. Representation in Wales changed less. Even here, however, the three extra county and two extra borough seats made electoral contests much more likely. In the important general election of 1830, not a single contest was held in the Principality. That would never happen after 1832.

Considered together, Catholic Emancipation and parliamentary reform produced dramatic changes in Ireland. Extending the vote to leaseholders in the counties in 1832 increased the electorate there from 26,000 to 61,000 [39]. In the boroughs, one adult Irishman in 13 could now vote. It is difficult to see how first Daniel O'Connell and later various groupings of nationalist politicians could have made the impact they did without these changes. However, because of the capricious effects of the so-called 'certification system' in Ireland, the country's real electorate tended to be considerably lower than those nominally entitled to vote – even before the famine (see pp. 130–1). In Belfast it was perhaps only one-third of those nominally qualified and in Dublin a half [62].

In Britain as a whole, at least four major changes occurred directly because of the 1832 Reform Act. Electors were now required to be on a register in order to be able to vote. In a famous, and well-publicised, speech at Merchant Taylor's Hall in 1838, Peel explained the importance of registering as many known supporters as possible. In the same year, he wrote to a colleague:

> The Reform Bill has made a change in the position of parties, and in the practical working of public affairs, which the author of it did not anticipate.
>
> There is a perfectly new element of political power – namely the registration of voters, a more powerful one than either the Sovereign or the House of Commons.
>
> That party is strongest in point of fact which has the existing registration in its favour. (H. J. Hanham, *The Nineteenth Century*, Cambridge University Press, 1969, p. 283)

Both parties recognised the importance of registration, as the formation of the Tory Carlton and the Whig Reform Clubs in 1832 and 1836 respectively attests. Local party agents rapidly appeared in the larger constituencies. With them, the business of professionalising politics began in earnest.

This in turn produced another important consequence of 1832. It became increasingly difficult for an MP to retain that previously coveted label: 'Independent'. Party polarisation had been increasing since the late eighteenth century, but this process accelerated dramatically after 1832, influenced also by the large number of general elections fought during the so-called 'decade of reform'. Though elections only had to be called once every seven years, the extraordinary combination of two monarchical deaths, an unprecedented constitutional crisis and the appointment of a minority government which sought increased support through a fresh general election saw six fought in the space of 11 years. The intensity of debate polarised opinion. Many old-style independent county MPs saw the political advantage, and sometimes the financial necessity, of accepting a party label – usually Tory or Conservative.

Reform was also a distinctive triumph for the House of Commons. Both the Lords and, to a lesser extent, the crown had to be coerced into a measure they feared and distrusted. Parliamentary reform accelerated the important process whereby the levers of power shifted from Lords to Commons. For many radical MPs, indeed, 1832 represented the final triumph of 'the people' over a corrupt and corrupting court. As Francis Place told a reform meeting in Huddersfield: 'The Reform Bills will be of little value in themselves, except that they will be the commencement of the practical mode of breaking up the old rotten system' [39 p. 200]. A reformed Commons would also be a more effective guardian of the public purse, endorsing low-taxation policies in the interests of the nation as a whole. In this way, reform represented a direct and powerful link with mid-Victorian *laissez-faire* [70].

At the same time, the function of general elections began to change. Since 1714, no general election had directly resulted in a change of government, though a few had confirmed the monarch's choice of ministers. After 1832, the continued reduction of monarchical power and the growing professionalisation of politics ensured that both electorate and parties understood that the purpose of a general election was now to choose a government. That of 1841 was a watershed. It was the first time for well over a hundred years that one government with a working majority was replaced by another on the verdict of the voters. Thus even by the early 1840s, politics had a more recognisably modern feel.

Perhaps the most radical short-term shift in the political structure, however, affected not central but local government. The Municipal Corporations Act of 1835 would not have been enacted by a Tory government. High on the agenda of the reformist Whigs, who expected to gain politically, this Act revolutionised urban politics. The old self-elected corporations, often controlled by Tory landowners, began to be dismantled, to be replaced by ratepayer-elected borough councils. Here, at least, the Chartist cry for annual elections was met once a borough had decided to avail itself of the opportunities presented by the new legislation. The middle-class radical and anti-Corn Law campaigner Richard Cobden explained the new opportunities. A rate-payer franchise, he somewhat disingenuously asserted, could secure 'to all classes a share in [the] government and protection [of the borough]; give unity, force, efficiency to the intelligent and wealthy community of Manchester, and qualify it by organisation, as it is already entitled by numbers, to be the leader in the battle against monopoly and privilege. In a word, INCORPORATE YOUR BOROUGH' [5 p. 83].

It was not surprising that the young Benjamin Disraeli, then no lover of the moneyed and commercial classes, should have been so opposed to the new legislation: 'The reform of the municipal corporations of England is a covert attack on the authority of the English gentry' [5 pp. 163–4]. Disraeli, with characteristic shrewdness, saw that the advance of municipal government would disadvantage the Tories and advance the interests of those whom he called 'Liberal oligarchs'. In municipal reform, more than anywhere else, we can see how the consequences of the 1832 Reform Act, in the words of that highly misleading cliché, 'gave power to the middle classes'. In Leeds, as in many other large boroughs, party rivalries were usually keener over local rather than national issues [55]. The outcome of borough elections was likely to have much more direct impact on the lives of the citizens, through policies on sewerage, drainage and a range of public amenities.

More nebulous, but just as important, the passage of the Reform Act was the single most important factor in the creation of what we might call a culture of reform in the 1830s and 1840s. The Whigs having created a propertied electorate on a more uniform basis than before, both they and their Tory successors after 1841 showed themselves directly responsive to propertied opinion both on the land and in the towns. The Grey government of 1830–34 removed some 1,500 court and government positions and its net income fell by 13 per cent. As Harling notes, 'taxpayers enjoyed practically all the savings, for the Whigs chose to use surplus revenue to reduce taxes rather than service the national debt' [39 p. 218].

Not for nothing have historians called the 1830s the 'decade of reform'. The results of the 1832 general election gave a majority for the abolition of slavery in the British empire in 1833. There followed a range of reforms designed either to remove abuses or to make government cheaper or more efficient, or both. In addition to Municipal Corporations, the 1830s saw a major reform of the poor law (from which ratepayers were the main beneficiaries), a series of church reforms and new legislation for county police forces following Peel's famous metropolitan police legislation of 1829. Significantly, much of this legislation was supported by the mainstream of both political parties. Legislation gave MPs more work to do. The length of the parliamentary year, which only rarely exceeded a leisurely five months during the eighteenth century, increased significantly.

The Great Reform Act was passed with conservative intentions. Government should remain in the hands of great landowners. Both parties recognised, however, that the price for this was to kill the damaging charge that government was merely part of 'Old Corruption'. The true measure of the 1832 Reform Act, therefore, is not to be gauged by the number of new voters or in 'giving power to the middle classes' but in the tacit new partnership between government and governed. Wellington and Croker were as right to be fearful of the long-term impact of the Great Reform Act as they were wrong in their diagnosis of its immediate consequences.

PART THREE: REDEFINING THE 'PRIVILEGED PALE OF THE CONSTITUTION'

5 NO 'FINAL SOLUTION', 1832–65

THE REFORM PARTY AT WESTMINSTER IN THE 1840s AND 1850s

In the autumn of 1837 Lord John Russell was being harried in the House of Commons by a number of radical MPs. They called for further political reform, particularly a secret ballot and shorter parliaments, and they accused the government of backstairs deals with the Tory opposition to preserve the old order. Their analysis was truer than the Whig government could admit and Russell was stung into over-reaction. He told his tormentors that they could expect no further reform [66 p. 123].

Russell, though a believer in the aristocratic principle of 'government by the best', did not, in truth, believe what he had said. Indeed, in another part of the speech made in parliament on 20 November he made his true position clear: 'Do I then say that the measure is in all respects final? I say no such nonsense'. No matter. He immediately earned the nickname 'Finality Jack'. For how long could it sensibly be maintained that further reform was neither necessary nor desirable? In one sense, it was easier for the political elite to hold the line when confronted by the unequivocally democratic challenge of the Chartists [60; 67]. At the end of his life 'Orator' Hunt pointed the way: 'There are seven millions of men in the United Kingdom, who are rendered so many *political outlaws* by the Reform Bill; by the provisions of that Act, they are to all intents and purposes so many political slaves' [22 p. 274]. Chartism was the response. This major topic has generated an enormous literature but a movement by, and on behalf of, those who had been excluded from direct representation in 1832 offers no clues as to the timing of future changes in the representative system. Chartist petitions were rejected by huge majorities in the Commons in 1839 and 1842, and the threat of confrontation (if not outright revolution) in 1848 – though taken seriously by the authorities – only consolidated parliament behind a position of 'no surrender' to coercion. The threat posed by Chartism delayed parliamentary consideration of adjustments to the franchise and the distribution of seats.

Pressure for parliamentary reform slackened after the Chartist humiliation of 1848 but did not disappear. Most reformers in parliament remained rootedly opposed to the Chartists' democratic platform but a strong thread links the work of reformers before and after 1832, both inside parliament and outside. As Biagini and Reid have argued: 'there was a substantial continuity in popular radicalism throughout the nineteenth and into the twentieth century' [74 p. 1]. The reform campaigns of 1866–68 (see Chapter 6) did not come out of nothing. How significant they were is a matter of debate. Theo Hoppen's brisk denunciation – 'In the twenty years before 1865 the cause of franchise reform ... came at times to resemble nothing so much as a corpse on the dissecting table' [11 p. 237] – is surely too harsh. At the very least the corpse could twitch with some vigour.

A reform party was in continuous existence at Westminster. Those known to contemporaries as 'radicals and reformers' numbered between 40 and 50 in the late 1840s and early 1850s. They were linked uneasily with the Whigs and Liberals but often only in the negative sense of not being Tories. Within this group, about 20 gave parliamentary reform consistent priority. Many of them were from aristocratic backgrounds; some were extremely wealthy. They might most usefully be called 'radical parliamentary reformers' and they need to be clearly distinguished both from the Whig leadership (and particularly Lord John Russell) and local party activists whose reformist objectives, as we shall see, were rather different. The most senior radical reformer was the veteran Joseph Hume, but a number of others, like W. J. Fox, J. A. Roebuck and Thomas Perronet Thompson, had been staunch reformers since the 1820s. Many of them had written for the radical journal *Westminster Review* [70 pp. 25–7]. At a time when 'two-party politics' were less dominant following the split in the Tory party over the repeal of the Corn Laws in 1846, a small cohesive grouping could exercise considerable influence. The reformers did more than merely keep the reform question alive in the years following the collapse of Chartism. Hume produced bills for reform in every parliamentary session between 1848 and 1852. Two other reformers, Francis Berkeley and Peter Locke King, introduced measures designed to secure a secret ballot and an increase in the number of county MPs regularly during the 1850s.

As Miles Taylor has noted, the predominant interest of this doughty group was much more with the distribution of seats and the form of voting than with an increase in the franchise [70 *p. 163*]. This was no accident. Most radical reformers were no more 'democratic' in their views than was the Whig leadership. Many shared the view of the free-trader Richard Cobden that adding working-class voters to the existing system would do little or nothing to improve it. Unlike the Whigs, however, they were passionately concerned with the independence of the House of Commons and they sought to rescue it from the clutches of the executive. The radical reformers of the 1850s were in an important sense the political descendants of those who had sought in the 1770s to purge the constitution from the illegitimate influence of an overbearing monarch (Chapter 2). The battle for supremacy between legislature (parliament) and executive (the government – crown and ministers in the 1770s; the cabinet in the 1850s) was a long one. As we know, it would eventually be won resoundingly by the executive. Chafing in opposition in the mid-1970s, Lord Hailsham, a leading Conservative spokesman, called the British system of government an 'elective dictatorship' controlled by a powerful prime minister. Thereafter a still more powerful Conservative one, Margaret Thatcher, proceeded to centralise it further throughout the 1980s – and Hailsham, though garrulous and unguarded on most topics, now kept quiet on this.

Since the dream of the House of Commons as pure, undefiled and maintaining close control over the executive would elude the radical parliamentary reformers of the 1850s, their contribution to the history of reform has been underplayed. That they would be defeated was far from clear at the time. For them, cleansing the political system of 'corruption' and 'influence' remained the key priority. Intellectual, professional and many other middle-class reformers tended to concentrate on those elements in the People's Charter most likely to advance this objective: equal electoral districts and a secret ballot [*Doc. 8*].

These reformers' other priority was cheap government. This, too, goes against the grain of a conventional historiography which links reform with the onward march of state power as the means whereby the ills of the poor were redressed. On this interpretation, as parliamentary reform extends the numbers of voters, so the tentacles of the state extend to provide first factory, public health and local government reform and later old-age pensions, school meals for the needy and national insurance. Such services, of course, require a larger and more vigorous executive supported by a professionalised civil service [6]. Parliamentary reform and the growth of government thus seem to go hand in hand.

This was so only in a chronological sense. The link between cause and effect was much more tenuous. Some of the most consistent parliamentary reformers of the first half of the nineteenth century were also among the strongest advocates of low taxation and cheap government. The reason for this demonstrates the importance of continuity in the history of parliamentary reform. The radical parliamentary reformers believed that a government which kept taxes low would also be a government with fewer oppressive powers and with fewer opportunities to reward the unworthy with political favours. The balance between legislature and executive would be tilted, as the reformers wanted, in favour of the former. Old Corruption would be dealt a mortal blow. Only with the benefit of hindsight might we conclude that the reformers were fighting irrelevant old battles. From the perspective of the 1850s, it was far from clear that government was capable of understanding, still less acting upon, a concept of national interest which a majority of members of the House of Commons would accept.

The conflict between pragmatism and purity was clear enough. Those Liberal activists who favoured parliamentary reform were much more concerned with its party political implications than were radicals of the Hume and Locke King stamp. Radical parliamentary reformers wanted uniformly large constituencies in which the importance of public opinion would be given full weight. Activists looked more carefully at the balance of political advantage. The Leeds newspaper proprietor and Liberal supporter, Edward Baines, warned in the *Leeds Mercury* in 1848 that equal electoral districts would produce an unhelpful amalgam of rural and urban voters in large constituencies [70 p. 170]. These would be anyway difficult to organise and held the real danger that the predominantly Liberal sympathies of the urban voter would be swamped by 40-shilling freeholders in the surrounding countryside. In one area, the county franchise, purity and pragmatism came together. Encouraged by the important changes which had been made in Ireland in 1850 (see p. 131), Russell and Locke King were convinced of the need to increase the numbers of voters in rural areas. They calculated that householders and perhaps the smaller tenant farmers also would help to reduce the inbuilt Conservative majority in many county seats.

Whig supporters were uncomfortably aware that the number of working-class voters (who tended in most places to vote Whig rather than Tory) was actually dwindling in many of the more open pre-1832 boroughs as old-qualified working men died off. The Whig/Liberal leadership had another concern. Cleaning up in large urban constituencies like Birmingham, Sheffield and Leeds was all very well but it was nowhere near sufficient to produce a parliamentary majority. The Whigs needed to win back strength in the counties which had been whittled away by Peel's Conservatives after 1832. They also needed to hang on to the kind of small boroughs which the radical parliamentary reformers would have removed without a second thought. The substantial recovery which the Liberals recorded in both types of seat at the 1857 general election reflects in part growing prosperity from which an incumbent Liberal government under Palmerston benefited and in part the hard work of local party managers who would have been extremely disconcerted had the agenda of the radical parliamentary reformers been taken up.

Rationalisations for conservatism could always be found. Gladstone remarked in 1859 that the continued existence of a number of 'managed' boroughs was important to enable talented young men to take seats in parliament in their early twenties, as he had done, and serve a valuable political apprenticeship. The Whigs became increasingly sensitive to party political advantage and it is significant that during the course of Russell's fidgety proposals to adjust the franchise in the 1850s and early 1860s (see Chronology), the number of small boroughs he proposed to remove was reduced in number.

As so often with reforming movements, the impetus of parliamentary reform during the 1850s was lessened by conflict and divisions between the protagonists. The radical political reformers had, no doubt, the purer motives; the Whigs wanted to continue governing the country. Meanwhile the Conservatives, who formed minority administrations in 1852 and 1858–59, were alive to the possibility that judicious adjustments on the franchise question could be made to work to their advantage and even help to lift what was beginning to seem the perpetual gloom of minority status. Party politicians, therefore, had equal reason for persisting with parliamentary reform. As the Chronology indicates (pp. 124–6), four developed proposals – three Whig and one Conservative – were presented to parliament in the years 1852–60. Additionally, with the abolition of property qualifications for MPs in 1858, the first of the six points of the People's Charter reached the statute book.

'A GOOD PROOF OF PRUDENCE': ENFRANCHISING THE RESPECTABLE

The party leaders gave a much higher priority to increasing the numbers of voters than did the radical parliamentary reformers. They had two main objectives. The first, and less important, was to reduce the anomalies left by the arrangements made in 1832. The second was to increase the number of 'respectable' voters. Since virtually all of what might be called the middle ranks in society had been enfranchised in 1832, this now meant giving the vote to respectable working men. Respectability was a key term in Victorian Britain. It denoted a degree of economic independence, such as could be enjoyed by those who had a secure job bringing in decent wages. It encompassed at least outward conformity to Church or Chapel; most branches of nonconformity were by the 1850s eminently, if not oppressively, respectable. More vaguely, but arguably most important of all, it indicated a willingness to play by the existing social rules. The respectable were expected to be organised, thrifty and prudent. They kept up with their rent. They would put away surplus cash in savings banks; they were members of friendly societies which offered insurance benefits at times of need; they would be members of burial clubs, thus avoiding the ultimate stigma of a pauper's grave. They would not blow what their families could not afford in the pub or at the racecourse. Above all, they were not what contemporaries dismissively termed 'the residuum': the unemployed, or casually employed whose behaviour was characterised by the reverse of all the virtues outlined above – with plenty of petty thievery thrown in. The carnality and criminality of society's all-too-obvious outsiders were perceived to pose such a threat that the 'residuum' shaded imperceptibly into the 'dangerous classes'.

The dichotomy which the Victorians set up between 'respectable' and 'residuum' was crude, stereotypical and insensitive. They also felt it to be real and important. Moreover, many working people accepted it without demur. Most of them were, after all, much more directly vulnerable to the predations of the 'dangerous' than were the prosperous middle classes who could afford to live at a safe distance from the 'roughs'. There is no evidence whatsoever that the majority of working men in the 1850s and early 1860s sought universal manhood suffrage. The retreat from the first point of the Charter was substantial and, among the political elite, clearly noted. The decline in mass protest, precipitous after the Kennington Common débâcle in 1848, was a crucial factor in persuading politicians that respectable working men could be trusted with the vote.

Lord John Russell talked in 1853 of enfranchising only those who had given 'a good proof of prudence' [11 p. 239]. Precisely how this distinction was to be carried through into legislation was a ticklish question. It was not feasible to include a 'respectability questionnaire' as part of the paraphernalia of the decennial censuses. Nor could a mid-nineteenth-century government, unlike its equally moralistic late twentieth-century counterpart, set up an 'education for citizenship' programme. In any case, respectable working men, by reading newspapers, attending Mechanics' Institutes and the like, were proving at least as well informed on the key questions of the day as were their supposed 'betters'. The sober sagacity of those working men with whom William Gladstone permitted himself to come into contact during two lengthy tours – of Bradford, Middlesborough and other industrial cities of the north-east in 1862 and of the north-west in 1864 – was a key factor in converting the future prime minister to franchise reform. Long since converted from the rooted hostility he espoused in 1830–32, he had nevertheless been noticeably lukewarm during the 1850s [Doc. 10]. In 1859, for example, he expressed a preference for keeping the franchise as it was. Existing voters showed appropriate 'willingness to defer to others more competent [and who showed] respect for the established order' [68 p. 389].

The only feasible solution, and an appropriately Victorian one, was financial. The £10 household rental qualification in the boroughs was agreed by nearly all reformers to set too high a hurdle. Russell proposed to reduce it in 1852, 1854 and 1860 to £6. The Conservatives, not yet converted to the electoral value of working-class votes and calculating that they would only be enfranchising more Liberal voters in the boroughs, retained the 1832 borough threshold in their 1859 bill (see p. 125). Their proposals were, however, innovative in other ways. They intended to equalise the borough and county rental qualification and give the vote to the posher type of lodger. They also took further the idea, unveiled by Russell and the Liberals in 1854, of what were called 'fancy franchises': votes for those who had £60 in a savings bank, were in receipt of government pensions worth at least £20 a year, were professionally qualified as lawyers, doctors, ministers of religion or who held a university degree. Most of this privileged flotsam and jetsam would long since have qualified for the vote by other means and their attention-attracting presence in a Conservative reform bill almost certainly reflected the burgeoning presentational skills of Benjamin Disraeli. While speaking on the bill, Disraeli also became the first major statesman openly to state that democracy would not bring civilisation crashing about the ears of property owners: 'I have no apprehension myself that if you had manhood suffrage tomorrow the honest, brave and good natured people of England would resort to pillage, incendiarism and massacre'. He was careful to leave MPs in no doubt, however, that a government based on the democratic principle would not rest on secure foundations [76].

None of the four specific proposals got anywhere, though the Conservative bill failed by only 39 votes in a full House of Commons. Two had important political consequences. Russell was convinced that the unwelcome nature of his franchise proposals in 1852 reduced his popularity among the more conservative Whig/Liberal MPs (though they were not short of other reasons to consider him an irritation) and contributed to the fall of his government. Derby used the narrow failure of the 1859 proposals as an opportunity to ask the Queen to dissolve parliament. The ensuing general election brought the 75-year-old Viscount Palmerston into government yet again and Gladstone into a Liberal Cabinet for the first time.

By the early 1860s, parliamentary reform was simmering away, without ever threatening to take fire. The events of 1859 and 1860 had shown that it retained its ability to split parties. The Conservative bill provoked the resignations from Cabinet of the Home Secretary Spencer Walpole and the President of the Board of Trade, Joseph Warner Henley. Lord John Russell agreed to serve in Palmerston's Liberal government only on the promise that time would be found for the introduction of another reform bill. Palmerston, anything but a reformer by temperament, sighed inwardly; Russell's stipulation did nothing to salve the festering relations between Queen Victoria's two 'terrible old men'. Russell and Gladstone had a spat in 1860 over whether reform or the budget should take precedence. Some of these difficulties had their origins in personal vanity. They did, however, reflect a more general unease among the rank and file of both parties. Though parliamentary reform never left the political agenda in these years, it remained for most MPs an unwelcome intruder into the even tenor of mid-Victorian parliamentary business.

6 TOWARDS REFORM, 1865–68: THE CAUSES OF THE 'LEAP IN THE DARK'

LIBERAL PROPOSALS AND LIBERAL OPPOSITION

We have seen that, although it retained its zealous advocates, reform could hardly claim priority within the parliamentary timetable. Why, in the absence of anything resembling the scale of extra-parliamentary protest seen in 1830–32, did it so suddenly assume such prominence in the mid-1860s? A number of explanations are possible, but the most important reason was almost certainly the death of Palmerston in 1865. Though almost 82, his death was unexpected and it brought Russell back to the prime ministership. One old man notably averse to parliamentary reform was succeeded by another who obstinately (irrationally, his many detractors said) retained a boyish enthusiasm for it. The immensely experienced Liberal Cabinet minister, Sir Charles Wood, prophesied accurately enough as he walked away from Palmerston's funeral: 'Our quiet days are over; no more peace for us' [7 *p. 360*].

Cautiously, and with many contrary voices, Liberalism had been edging towards parliamentary reform for several years before Palmerston's death. The Rochdale Quaker, John Bright, now MP for Birmingham, lost no opportunity to press the reform case in the early 1860s. He suggested that Birmingham, with its multiplicity of small trades and artisans who worked in them, pointed the way to class collaboration and harmony. Working men could safely be entrusted with the vote. More significantly, Gladstone had been persuaded [*Doc. 10*] (see Chapter 5). After his unequivocal declaration in the Commons in May 1864, the cause of parliamentary reform could not be characterised within the Liberal party as the preserve only of a few idiosyncratic radicals and zealots, plus, of course, Lord John Russell.

Perhaps paradoxically, in view of the hectic events of 1866–68, it was the Liberal party which mattered. Its support in the early and mid-1860s was widespread. It encompassed both the landed aristocracy and the aristocracy of labour, while it claimed predominant allegiance from a wide range of middle ranks and dissenters [86]. The 1865 general election, which the party won with a majority of about 80 over the Conservatives, was the fifth successive occasion on which the Liberals had won more seats than their main opponents since the repeal of the Corn Laws in 1846 had shattered Tory unity. The Liberals were entrenched as the natural party of government. Continued political success depended, however, upon consensus over a range of policies acceptable to this breadth of interest and income. Exclusion of an artisan class, which in the 1850s and early 1860s showed every sign of accepting the beneficence of the existing political order, was not only insensitive; it looked increasingly to be bad politics [Doc. 11].

Liberalism was also a reformist creed in the wider sense. One reason for the broad base of support enjoyed by the Liberal party was that a wide range of reformist causes could find a home within it. Parliamentary reform was by no means dominant in this. Among a very large list were the Anti-Slavery Society, the Liberation Society (which campaigned against the excessive power and privileges of the Church of England), the United Kingdom Alliance (for temperance reform), movements for improved public health provision, a growing campaign for land reform and a rash of organisations aimed at increasing educational standards among the people. Most of these had cross-class appeal. Some were the key issues in local politics, uniting middle-class nonconformists and aspirant working men in a series of campaigns for 'improvement'. For these too, the death of the cynical populist Palmerston was a liberation. The stage seemed set in late 1865 for the dominant party of the age to grasp its reformist destiny without trimming or equivocation.

Recent events outside Britain also helped to confirm the importance of reform as a moral issue [59; 65; 74; 136]. Large gatherings turned out to celebrate the achievements of the Italian nationalist leader Garibaldi in 1862. Italian unification was a cause which united many diverse strands within Liberalism. Almost as popular was support for the North against the slave-owning South in the American Civil War of 1861–65. Anti-slavery worked against the economic interests of many cotton workers in the North-west, since so much of their raw material was imported from the southern states of the USA. The stoical victory of principle over self-interest did much to convince Gladstone that these were men who were indeed patient 'under suffering', demonstrated 'self-command' and who fulfilled his stringent moral criteria for coming 'within the pale of the Constitution' [Doc. 10]. The link between general reformist issues and the specific question of parliamentary reform was strengthening all the time. In 1864 and 1865, respectively, a middle-class Reform Union and a Reform League organised largely by skilled workers were founded to press for changes in the franchise. The main League objective was a household franchise, though the vote should also be extended to respectable lodgers. The League was not overtly 'democratic' and shared at least some of the fears of the middle classes about the 'residuum' (see Chapter 5).

With Russell as prime minister, parliamentary reform took priority. The problem for the post-Palmerston Liberal party, however, was that a broadly reformist stance on a wide range of issues masked rooted objection to specific proposals on most of them. Parliamentary reform was particularly tricky. Consensus, of a sort, existed on the proposition that something needed to done. Precisely what, however, was bound to be contentious. There was the further problem that detailed discussion on rental values in counties and boroughs was a massive turn-off for the majority of the population. The 1865 election had certainly not been dominated by parliamentary reform, as those of 1830–32 had been (see Chapter 3). The humorous magazine *Punch* was drawing on the experience of the past 15 years (see Chapter 5) when it published a cartoon of John Bull and his wife being sent to sleep by reading yet more speeches on parliamentary reform [86 *p. 210*].

Russell was aware of the problems. He would have preferred to have a Royal Commission investigate the arcane details of rental qualifications and their implications in particular seats. He would then act on its recommendations at leisure much later in the life of the 1865 parliament. Political balance required a radical presence in government. The Bradford Quaker, W. E. Forster, given a Cabinet post because Gladstone would not tolerate the presence of the more senior and much more forthright John Bright, pressed for immediate action and Russell was anxious not to alienate the northern industrial districts. The parliamentary party was, therefore, catapulted into considering a specific bill before the various interest groups could be properly consulted, still less squared.

The result, at least in hindsight, was predictable. The 1866 bill, which Gladstone attempted to pilot through the Commons, was not remotely radical. The proposed voting changes (see p. 125) would have added perhaps 200,000 borough voters to the electoral roll, most of them skilled working men. In the counties, about 170,000 new voters would be enfranchised by a substantial reduction of the rating qualification. The main beneficiaries here would have been professionals and business people working in the cities who had bought property in the adjacent countryside. Many of them, it was estimated, were loyal Liberal voters. The redistribution of seats proposed was also modest, for reasons both of party and principle. Those who had made a detailed study of changes in the franchise between the two Reform Acts remarked that, while many of the borough seats had developed in anticipated ways, growing prosperity had created an ever larger number of voters whose main source of income was urban but who had acquired the vote in county constituencies.

The calculations were designed to give maximum benefit to the Liberals, but they would not do. Those Liberals who had owed their allegiance before 1865 to Palmerston rather than to Russell felt bounced into a measure they distrusted by a minister they disliked. High-flown rationalisations were not slow in coming. Many of the Liberal opponents of reform, whom John Bright dubbed the 'Adullamites' (using a metaphor from the Old Testament to describe those who cowered in a dark cave of ignorance; they were also called 'the Cave' by contemporaries), were highly able men. Perhaps the ablest of the lot was Robert Lowe. Described – memorably if too harshly – by one historian as 'that sour invigilator of cant' [2 *p. 181*], he employed some arguments remarkably similar to those of the Tories in 1830–31. He suggested that the bill would weaken the representative nature of parliament and subject it to unwelcome pressures based on class identity rather than national interest.

Lowe also alleged that the influence of working people in the political system would produce growing pressure for higher taxes in order to improve social and environmental conditions. Liberal economic policy, of course, was rooted in cheap government, low taxation and *laissez-faire*. His attacks on the 'venality' and 'ignorance' of working people were crudely stereotypical. They also blithely ignored the fact that growing prosperity in the 1850s and early 1860s had produced an increasing number of working-class voters, especially in the large boroughs. These new voters, perhaps 25 per cent of the total electorate by the mid-1860s, hardly revealed themselves as dangerous revolutionaries. Lowe's collective insult produced a spirited response from reformers outside Westminster who organised meetings to demonstrate against the disgraceful travesty he offered. One speaker at a West Riding meeting in 1866 said that 'he stood there to tell the country that he was not, as Mr. Lowe had said he was, a drunken man, a venal man, or a man who intimidated his fellows' [59 *p. 265*].

The Adullamite leaders, who included important aristocratic figures such as Grosvenor, Lansdowne and the ex-Peelite Lord Elcho as well as Lowe, opened up deep fissures within the Liberal party in both houses. In these circumstances, it was necessary only for the Conservatives to remain united and the bill was lost. In case any independent-minded Tories were inclined to support it on the grounds that the Liberals might easily have come up with something far worse, Benjamin Disraeli had the appropriate riposte. Like it or loathe it, it would still be a *Liberal* bill. He had other plans, which would put his own party centre stage for the first time in 20 years.

A CONSERVATIVE BILL WHICH DID NOT CONSERVE

The Conservatives got their chance when an amendment to the bill was carried and Russell resigned, rather than asking the Queen to dissolve a parliament barely a year old. Why did the Conservatives take up what seemed to be the poisoned chalice of parliamentary reform in 1866? It was, after all, clear that most of their backbenchers were no keener on a large injection of working-class voters than were the Adullamites. Following the influential study by Maurice Cowling, most historians have been inclined to agree that, unlike 1832, the Second Reform Act owed little to extra-parliamentary pressure: 'In explaining the fact that an Act was passed in 1867 which went farther than any bill could have done at the end of 1865, we must examine the varying impacts made by the movement of events on the major political leaders' [75 p. 289]. Certainly, a powerful set of causal factors can be offered which relate more or less exclusively to the high politics in which Cowling's historiography is steeped. For a minority Conservative administration to succeed in highly controversial legislation which had tripped the Liberals up would be an immense boost to Derby, now embarked on his third brief stint as prime minister, and Disraeli, who eyed the succession ever more covetously as his chief aged. A successful Conservative bill would raise morale both at Westminster and in the constituencies. Derby seems to have realised the possibilities earlier than Disraeli. He later told a colleague that 'he did not intend for a third time to be made a mere stop-gap until it should suit the convenience of the Liberals to forget their dissensions. ... I determined that I would ... convert, if possible, an existing minority into a practical majority ... carrying a measure ... the agitation for which was standing in the way of every measure ... of practical legislation' [92 p. 134].

Moreover, the Conservatives had long chafed at the inbuilt Liberal bias of the existing system. This had been intentionally fashioned by the Whigs when they themselves returned to office in 1830 after a long period in the wilderness. In particular, the insidious, and accelerating, infiltration of the county electorates by predominantly Liberal professional and industrial interests was widely held to disadvantage the Conservatives, who could usually be sure of holding seats in which genuinely rural interests predominated. The opportunity to correct – perhaps even over-correct – the balance in a Conservative bill appealed. Though the Conservatives were in a minority in the Commons, Disraeli calculated that sufficient radicals would support any bill which significantly increased the number of voters to secure a majority there. Moreover, the Conservatives appeared to be less frightened than the Liberals of that full 'household suffrage' favoured by the Reform League without fussy restrictions on rental values. Convinced reformers in parliament could hardly vote against a generous enhancement which they knew to be strongly supported outside Westminster merely because it appeared in Conservative, rather than Liberal, wrapping. Overall, then, the Conservatives had good reasons for thinking their gamble worthwhile.

But are such 'in-House' calculations sufficient to dispose of the argument that 1867 had little to do with extra-parliamentary pressure and threats of violence? The counter-example used by Royden Harrison in *Before the Socialists* (Routledge and Kegan Paul, 1965, *p. 133*) to suggest that Westminster was influenced by 'the proximity to revolutionary situations in 1866 and 1867' is not particularly persuasive in itself. The failure of the Liberal bill provoked some violence in Hyde Park in late July 1866. In May 1867 demonstrators defied a ban on holding a meeting there, requiring the authorities to use force to keep them out. In October 1866, a group of Sheffield saw grinders, who were on strike, attempted to blow up the house of a fellow worker who had refused to support their action. This incident, and others which followed it in 1867 collectively known as the 'Sheffield Outrages', were widely reported and led to detailed enquiries. All forms of coercion were contrary to that emphasis on freedom and mutual tolerance which lay at the core of Liberal radicalism [74 *p. 87*]. Enquiries into trade union violence did more to embarrass the Reform League, whose Secretary was the bricklayers' leader George Howell, than it did to influence Disraeli. Similarly, the development of Fenianism in Ireland had little direct impact. The rising in Ireland in 1867 was an 'ignominious defeat' [92 *p. 463*] and the famous Clerkenwell bombings, part of a bungled attempt to release Fenian prisoners in London, took place in December after the Second Reform Act was on the statute book.

Reform was no panic response to coercion. Derby and Disraeli were not bowing to a process which it was beyond their power to control. Extra-parliamentary pressure did have its effect, however. Liberal radical and working-class pressure had put parliamentary

reform firmly on the agenda by the middle of 1866. The failure of
Russell's initiative would not take it off again. The extent, and the co-
ordination, of reaction to that failure is worth stressing. Quite apart
from the overplayed Hyde Park incident, the summer of 1866 saw
major street demonstrations and protest meetings in a large number
of places, including Birmingham, Bristol, Norwich and Rochdale. The
Reform League provided the organisational impetus but the predominant mood of the skilled working classes was clear enough. 'In all
demonstrations anger and indignation featured prominently: the
workers wanted vindication of their moral character against the
charges of chronic drunkenness and depravity. Resolutions approved
at meetings … regularly placed great emphasis on the respectability of
the working classes' [59 pp. 262–3]. We may conclude that Disraeli
was able to grasp his great tactical opportunity in large part because
extra-parliamentary pressure had created the climate in which some
kind of reform was widely seen as inevitable.

But what kind? The 7th Earl of Shaftesbury wrote to Derby in
October 1866: 'a measure of Reform is indispensable. But you can, I
am sure, construct one, extensive, safe and satisfactory' [75 p. 119].
What the Conservative government finally enacted in August 1867
was certainly extensive but the gravest doubts existed on all sides as
to whether it was either safe or satisfactory. Little in the intervening
period was either pre-ordained or carefully planned. The original
intention was to play for time, partly to enable the scale of the Liberal
reverse to register at Westminster, partly to postpone the promotion
of a bill which might well have exactly the same end result as the Liberals' one. There was, yet again, talk of Royal Commissions and
mature, reflective consideration of weighty issues. By February 1867,
however, Derby had determined to press ahead with a bill.

The prime minister was, however, clear that the Conservatives
needed to offer more than the Liberals – or at least *appear* to do so.
He proposed a borough household suffrage entirely cynically: 'Of all
possible Hares to start I do not know a better' [77 p. 98]. He intended
to restrict its practical effect by limiting actual voting rights to those
who paid poor relief, had a two-year residence qualification and paid
their rates directly to the authorities, rather than indirectly as part of
rent to a landlord. Very many working men moved frequently
between rented properties and knew absolutely nothing about the
payment of rates. Derby's safeguards would restrict the electorate
much more than decisions about whether the vote should go to £6 or
to £7 householders. A 'complete' householder franchise would in
practice be much more restrictive than it seemed [Doc. 15].

The very idea of it, however, was too much for some senior Conservatives. In early March three Cabinet ministers resigned: Lord Cranborne, the Secretary for India and son of the Marquess of Salisbury, the Earl of Carnarvon, the Colonial Secretary, and General Jonathan Peel, War Secretary and younger brother of the late prime minister. All were horrified at the prospect of rough, ill-educated working men choosing members of a mature, deliberative assembly which legislated for a whole empire. Derby's ministry survived the defections, however, and Disraeli began to pilot the bill through the House of Commons. In its original form it contained Derby's safeguards against full household suffrage, buttressed by the return of a few 'fancy franchises' (see Chapter 5). In the counties, a high rental qualification of £15 was proposed to ensure that propertied county interests would be properly safeguarded. County boundaries were also to be redrawn with the aim of placing more urban voters into borough constituencies, where Conservatives were convinced they belonged.

Beyond being concerned with parliamentary reform, the Act bore hardly any other resemblance to the original bill [94]. Benefiting from widespread backbench feeling that reform was inevitable, Disraeli had two objectives: to ensure that a Tory bill got on to the statute book and to block every suggested amendment or 'improvement' which came from the Liberal leadership. His tactics have been widely praised. Robert Blake, in his famous biography *Disraeli* (Eyre & Spottiswoode, 1966) concluded that 'For what he did in 1867 he deserves to go down to history as a politician of genius' (p. 477). His exploits certainly confirmed him as Derby's natural successor to the party leadership and stilled (for a time at least) that insidiously unpleasant strain of anti-Semitism which has emerged periodically in the Tory party during the last century and a half. But was it truly 'genius'? Disraeli was, indeed, extremely adroit but praise for his tactics should not be unstinting. If he had no fixed opinion on the details of the bill provided it could get a Commons majority, if most Liberal radicals would support a measure which went further than Gladstone and Russell had been prepared to do and if most other MPs were resigned to reform anyway, then it did not need political 'genius' to succeed even without a Commons majority. The key to understanding Disraeli's success in the Commons in the spring of 1867 lies in three other factors not dependant on his own skills: the desperation of the Conservatives for success; the lack of understanding about the franchise which most backbench MPs had; and the relative weakness of party discipline before the 1870s. There were no three-line whips and

MPs were quite prepared to vote on important matters according to their consciences.

But what of the House of Lords, where there was certainly no natural majority for reform and where sat able and well-informed opponents like Carnarvon and Baron Cairns? Historians have devoted less attention to the upper house, but success there was equally vital. Derby worked skilfully in the Lords, exploiting divisions in the opposition and rallying peers loyal to the leadership with memories of what had happened to a previous Tory bill in 1859 (see Chapter 5). A number of amendments were attempted but only one succeeded. Disraeli's plan for redistributing parliamentary seats was modest but it did include giving a third member of parliament to the largest urban centres (see pp. 131–2). Baron Cairns introduced an amendment which precluded voters from using more than two votes. His intention was to ensure that the natural minority party (usually the Conservatives) would be able to secure one MP from the largest towns. This amendment passed the Lords with only limited opposition. When it reached the Commons, Gladstone attacked it roundly, enabling Disraeli to make it a party issue. Few Tories were keen on Cairns's amendment because it abandoned the basic principle that electors should be able to exercise as many choices as there were seats available. Worse, they felt that it established a wedge which might lead all the way to equal electoral districts (a particular fear of Gladstone's) and even to proportional representation, a complex notion favoured only by outlandish intellectuals like John Stuart Mill. Nevertheless, they answered Disraeli's rallying cry and voted against Gladstone. The so-called 'minority clause' was to have significant, if unintended, consequences in the 1870s (see Chapter 7).

Disraeli's 'triumph' in the Commons amounted to little more than abandoning all the safeguards against a wide borough franchise which the original bill had incorporated. Out went the 'fancy franchises' while the residence qualification was reduced from two years to one. Redistribution proposals were also changed, though the Conservatives were able to ensure that about 100,000 voters were transferred from county to borough seats, leaving many counties representing a larger proportion of genuinely rural interests. Much the most radical change, however, was the so-called 'Hodgkinson Amendment'. This abolished in parliamentary boroughs the practice of 'compounding', whereby landlords paid rates (for poor law and other charges) directly to the authorities on behalf of their tenants. The details are fearsomely complex and very few MPs had a working knowledge of rating law anyway, but most 'compounders' were the poorer tenants and Disraeli's acceptance of the amendment transformed the scope of the bill, adding perhaps 400,000 voters. This clause alone virtually doubled the existing borough franchise before other, less contentious, extensions were taken into account.

Disraeli accepted what was a poorly-drafted amendment (needing considerable later attention) because it did not have broad Liberal party support and especially because it would embarrass its leadership. A tighter rating amendment than Hodgkinson's was on offer from H. C. E. Childers but it was known that Gladstone intended to speak in its favour and Disraeli would not tolerate any kind of endorsement from the opposition front bench. Thus, Grosvenor Hodgkinson, a solicitor in Newark who had been elected to represent that borough as a Liberal at the general election of 1859 and who had remained in decent backbench obscurity thereafter, earned a permanent place at least in the footnotes of all textbooks on nineteenth-century political history. It was his amendment which made the Second Reform Act such a 'leap in the dark'.

Disraeli intended to postpone reform in Ireland indefinitely, offering the excuse that Fenian nationalist activity rendered major franchise changes unsafe there. A very pallid Reform Act was eventually passed in 1868, however, (see p. 133) which increased the borough franchise by about 50 per cent to 45,000 or so, in significant part because some county voters were now transferred to the boroughs. Scotland also had its own Reform Act in 1868 (see p. 132) which changed things a good deal more. The principles were broadly the same as those for England with the exception that no lodger franchise was needed. Under Scottish law, lodgers were legally tenants so that distinction had no force. Scotland received in 1868 what amounted to a householder franchise in the boroughs. This borough electorate consequently increased by almost three times; in England it slightly more than doubled. As in England, though, practicalities restricted the franchise. Those who did not pay rates could not vote, and this requirement alone disfranchised approximately two-thirds of the Irish householders in the borough of Glasgow [14 *p. 416*].

Disraeli was much more concerned about the redistribution of seats. In terms of population, Scotland was substantially under-represented in the UK parliament. Before 1867, it returned only 53 MPs when proportionality would have seen it entitled to approximately 90. There was the political problem, however, that since 1832 the country had been, in effect, a Whig–Liberal fiefdom. Disraeli was perfectly happy to add many more voters who just might change the balance. He was much less keen to add to an inbuilt Liberal majority

in the northern kingdom. Thus, redistribution did little to favour the
Scots. Only seven new seats were created, with a slight bias towards
the counties.

To the uncontrolled anger of some, the consternation of many, and
the wild-eyed surprise of almost all, then, the Conservatives piloted
major reform Acts through the Commons in 1867 and 1868. No one
could foresee how things would actually work out.

7 CONSEQUENCES: THE LEAP AND ITS AFTERMATH, 1867–80

HOW MUCH CHANGE?

Whatever the reservations in Westminster, the Second Reform Act was enthusiastically received outside. A large meeting was held in Manchester at which veterans of the Peterloo era, including the redoubtable Samuel Bamford, joined with Chartists and Reform Leaguers to celebrate a great triumph. The *Newcastle Weekly Chronicle* published a euphoric article, 'The Triumph of Reform':

> Great as were the effects the Reform Bill of 1832 produced we are perfectly satisfied that the Reform Bill of 1867 will produce still greater effects. Progress in all directions will presently be registered. Ignorance will give place to education, prejudice to justice, peace and good will to hostility and contempt ... a glorious future is before us. [*59 p. 277*]

Such a glowing testimony to the effects of Disraeli's cynicism and political calculation reads oddly nowadays. It was, however, a perfectly reasonable response from those, like the Reform League, who looked for 'progress' in human affairs and believed that the virtues of the respectable working man had finally received their just reward. From their perspective, it was entirely proper to concentrate on the secret ballot and equal electoral districts, rather than 'manhood suffrage' as the immediate future objectives [*Docs 15 and 18*]. Rural workers had not benefited from 1867. Few considered this a major injustice since agricultural labourers clearly needed more 'education' before they could either 'be entrusted with the suffrage' or be independent-minded enough to resist pressure from landlords or employing tenant farmers.

   If Disraeli hoped that the gratitude of skilled working men and the unity of a still bedazzled Conservative party would be sufficient to break the electoral hegemony of the Liberal party in the 1868 general election, he was to be sorely mistaken. In one sense, of course, the election was premature. The major changes he had brought took time to work their way through into the system and the electoral registers in the new boroughs, in particular, were far from complete by the time it was fought. Nevertheless, the verdict was unequivocal. The new voters combined with the old to give Disraeli a depressingly old message about Conservative electability. Gladstone was the name on all lips and the Liberals were installed with a majority of about 110, an advance on the already highly satisfactory outcome of the 1865 election. For Disraeli, the results from the boroughs were particularly depressing. The Conservatives suffered a net loss of 33 seats there as the Liberals seemed to confirm their reputation as the party of the people. Of the 114 seats with more than 50,000 electors only 25 were won by Conservatives. Things obstinately refused to improve in Scotland and Ireland, where net losses of eight and ten seats respectively left the Conservatives in a heavy minority. They won only eight seats out of 60 in Scotland [91 *p. 73*]. In the burghs they made virtually no impression whatever, winning only one seat (Ayr in 1874) in the three successive elections from 1868 to 1880 [132]. By contrast, the Conservatives almost enjoyed parity with the Liberals in England, trailing the Liberals by only 223 seats to 240.

On the surface, Derby's famous 'leap in the dark' had confirmed the black outlook for Conservatives. The respectable working men who had rushed to register their new entitlement in the boroughs were mostly thoroughgoing Gladstonian Liberals. Continuity, rather than change, seemed to be the electoral message from the radical changes of 1867. Most Conservative crumbs of comfort came in the traditional places. The party's showing in the English counties, where more members now sat (see p. 132) was more than respectable. The Tories won 60 per cent of county seats overall. The massive increase in the number of borough voters now ensured, however, that the counties were not under-represented in terms of population. The United Kingdom had 280 county seats (42.5 per cent of the total). R. D. Baxter's calculations for 1868 suggested that this was almost exactly proportional to the number of county voters (42.2 per cent).

If one digs deeper, however, a few early rumblings may be heard of the major volcanic eruption which would blast apart the hegemonic status of the Liberal party and establish the Conservatives as the natural party of government before the end of the century. London was a bright spot. The hated intellectual John Stuart Mill was turned out at Westminster by the newsagent W. H. Smith. A Tory was returned for the City of London for the first time since 1852 and also in Middlesex, where suburban voters carried the seat. In one or two places where the working-class electorate had risen most sharply, the Conservatives did surprisingly well. Blackburn, a Lancashire town with a strong tradition of factory paternalism, where 75 per cent of the electorate were working men, returned a Conservative [148].

Lancashire, indeed, was the jewel in an admittedly tarnished Tory crown in 1868. All eight county seats were won there and this included the highest-profile Liberal election defeat of all, Gladstone's in south-west Lancashire [142; 143]. The borough triumphs were yet more spectacular, since 'cotton Lancashire' had by 1868 been so strongly Liberal for so long. Twenty-four of the 36 Lancashire seats were in Conservative hands after the 1868 election. These included Liverpool and Stockport, where anti-Irish prejudice had long been a source of Tory strength. In certain Lancashire seats, as the *Ashton Reporter* put it in November 1868, the Conservatives had won because workers believed the radical Protestant, and Irish Unionist, message that 'we were on the verge of Popery ... unless measures were taken to arrest its progress, the Pope of Rome would be King of England' [82 *p.102*]. More surprisingly, both seats were won in Salford [143] and one in Manchester. Here, too, Irish Unionists were holding demonstrations and calling for popular support. In both places, the electorate had increased hugely after the Second Reform Act. Bemused Liberal strategists took an olympian but, as events would later prove, disastrously wrong-headed line in explaining these reverses. W. A. Abram's analysis included recent prosperity, which Conservative manufacturers were able to exploit to influence their workers. His main explanation, however, was the 'sluggishness of operative's reason' [91 *p. 67*]. This left them with a 'sheer inability to construe events'. Crudely, the new voters were not bright enough to understand why the Liberals were the natural home for the working man's vote.

These were more than straws in the wind. For those willing to look hard enough, the new voters, who included a very large number of men who did not fit the stereotype of the working man motivated by the spirit of thrift, self-denial and self-improvement, were not natural Liberals. The new votes had to be fought for. Though Gladstone (once he had found a new seat) emerged triumphant from the 1868 election, the Reform Acts would soon be seen to have put to an end a generation of what had become, in many quarters, complacent Liberal superiority. Widespread dissatisfaction at a Gladstone government widely perceived by voters to have been both too meddling (not least in the matter of dictating to drinkers when they could use licensed premises) and too much in pawn to radicals, dissenters and puritans, saw Disraeli into government in 1874 with a majority of almost 50 seats. The Liberals lost no fewer than 73 seats in England and 15 in Scotland [86 p. 272]. The Tories, as they had at their last election victory in 1841, dominated the English counties, winning 143 of the 170 seats available there. More interestingly, the suburban London vote consolidated behind the Conservatives. The Home Counties swung strongly towards the Tories, establishing a pattern which has been replicated in all strong Conservative years since [76; 87; 89]. The vote of the small property owner in southern England was sliding uncontrollably away from the Liberals [Doc. 19].

Compared with 1832, the expansion in the number of voters in 1867–68 was huge (see p. 136). According to the contemporary statistician Dudley Baxter, the total number of voters increased by about 83 per cent but particularly so in the boroughs where about 700,000 new voters were created. A number of industrial boroughs now had clear working-class majorities and some were transformed out of all recognition. Ten times as many men could vote in Merthyr Tydfil in 1868 as in 1866. Birmingham, already a substantial parliamentary borough with 15,500 voters in 1866, had 42,000 by 1869. The electorate of Leeds quadrupled in size; those of Stoke, Halifax, South Shields and Blackburn increased five-fold [140 p. 310].

POLITICAL ORGANISATIONS AND PARTY FORTUNES

The implications of all of this for political parties were soon clear. Political organisation in the towns was transformed [78]. Party clubs needed to become much more professional in order to 'collect, guide and control' the mass electorates which had emerged. Part of this process needed to be managed locally; other parts required central direction. A crucial element in the Conservative political revival was improved organisation from the centre under the guiding hand of John Eldon Gorst [Doc. 16], a barrister who had lost his parliamentary seat in 1868. The Tory emphasis was explicitly on building up first the interest, and then the loyalty, of working-class voters. Both parties gave much more attention to political organisation after 1867 and both, too, remodelled their structures after electoral defeat in 1868 and 1874 [Doc. 20].

Party organisation was not all about politics. As John Garrard has said, 'local political parties were ... more than just *electoral* or even *political* organisations' [77 p. 134]. Though it pained many puritanical radicals to admit it, politics was very much a minority pastime. Organisers needed to provide attractive options to engage, and retain, membership. Sir William Agnew remarked of Salford in the 1870s that there 'was a great number of people ... who appeared to stand between two opinions – they were neither milk nor water, but were sufficiently numerous to turn an election. ... [T]hey were more likely to be attracted by clubs than by any other means' [77 p. 135]. Hence, political associations held meetings in buildings where members could drink (either tea or beer according to taste and ideology) and smoke in convivial surroundings. One local Conservative club regularly held concerts of 'popular and patriotic compositions'. They organised picnics and trips to the seaside or to spa towns. They involved the whole family. They offered fun in the hope of gaining loyalty.

Such solicitations, of course, came at a cost. The price paid by many ordinary MPs for continued support from the party was loyalty to an agreed slate of policies and to the party leadership. It is important not to exaggerate the totality of this development, or to suggest that it was *caused* by parliamentary reform. Clear party identification is discernible in the 1830s and 1840s and rules of party discipline which might bind MPs with limited means were usually slackened in the case of very wealthy, or aristocratically-connected, colleagues well after the 1870s. Nevertheless, 1867 did accelerate an important process. The loyalty of ordinary MPs towards their party was increasingly considered more important than individual opinion and conscience. Parties were being professionalised and professionalism implied control. The number of genuinely independent MPs had declined substantially after the first Reform Act. After the second, party strategists and outside observers increasingly assumed regular attendance at Westminster and a decent voting record on the right side. This was reflected in the sharply declining number of reverses on issues of policy which governments experienced. It was normal to lose 10 or 15 a year in the 1850s. By the 1890s, governments were going through sessions without losing more than one or two [17 p. 20]. The two-party system was reinforced. As the satirist and dramatist W. S. Gilbert put it in the operetta *Iolanthe* in 1882,

ev'ry boy and every gal that's born into this world alive, is either a little Liberal, or else a little Conservative.

The members on whom this increased party discipline operated were, however, from much the same social groups as before. Just before the first Reform Act, in 1831, it was calculated that 24 per cent of MPs were bankers, merchants and manufacturers; exactly the same proportion was elected in 1874 [11 p. 258]. While the proportion of professional middle-class MPs (solicitors, writers and the like) increased over this period, the House as a whole remained landowner-dominated. Landowners were likely to represent the smaller boroughs which remained such a feature of the post-1867 House of Commons and they monopolised the county seats. No significant change in the overall composition of the Commons occurred until the late 1880s.

The other main discontinuity confronting MPs after 1867 was 'public opinion'. Politicians needed to get to grips with this elusive, but increasingly important, concept. The role of newspapers, both as reflectors of public opinion and mouthpieces of party policy, assumed greater prominence as literacy levels grew. Fewer than four hundred provincial newspapers were published in 1858; there were more than nine hundred in 1874 [86 *p. 169*]. Some candidates grudgingly acknowleged that electors were more interested in their party allegiance than their personal qualities as politicians. Increasingly, voters judged between what were presented as the polarised views of Gladstone and Disraeli on such diverse issues as taxation, educational opportunity, whether rights to drink in licensed premises should be more tightly regulated and Britain's role in European and world affairs. The party leaders debated a range of political, religious and moral issues and presented them directly to the electorate. By the end of the 1870s, Gladstone was embarked on a series of what might today be called 'meet-the-people' speaking tours. Newspapers and party organisations were also beginning to be 'image-conscious'. New technology aided the portrayal of leading party figures in poses designed to be authoritative and persuasive. This was the age of the 'Gladstone mug' and, as a reflection of what good Liberals thought of him, the 'Disraeli chamber pot'. The Primrose League, founded by progressive Conservatives in the early 1880s to propagate not only the memory but the policies of Disraeli, was named after his favourite flower.

Increasingly, also, the verdict of the electorate was accepted without question. Disraeli broke with tradition in 1868 when he resigned before meeting parliament after the Conservatives' defeat. Gladstone repaid the compliment in 1874; Disraeli reciprocated again in 1880. Increasingly, political affairs were being determined by 'the people', or at least that significant minority of it which had the vote. The number of uncontested elections went down after 1832 but more candidates were usually being returned unopposed than had actually won an election: 383 out of 658 in 1859, for example. The number was down to 212 by 1868, to 109 in 1880 and only 43 in 1885 [89]. This was to be the lowest figure before the First World War, however. Elections after 1867 were about informing electors about party policy, knocking the opposition and choosing governments. They were no longer primarily about determining which *individual* MPs would represent a constituency. The change in political culture was very marked.

A RESPECTABLE ELECTORATE?

Despite worries about 'leaps in the dark', politicians in 1867 felt that, for better or worse, they had a reasonably clear idea about the *type* of voter they had enfranchised. The £12 franchise in the counties was intended by the Conservatives to keep those seats safe for property owners, which it very largely did – to the Tories' advantage. The number of English county voters increased by 45 per cent and in the United Kingdom as a whole by only 38 per cent. In the boroughs, despite an increase of about 138 per cent, the widespread assumption was that only the respectable, reflective end of the working class had been enfranchised. Disraeli could claim his bill as a 'bulwark against democracy' [92 *p. 233*]. Dunbabin concluded that, given the various important omissions 'the borough franchise was household, *not* manhood' [77 *p. 102*].

What was the reality? Research [140] has revealed a much more complex picture. Precisely who should qualify for the borough vote was not at all clear to the electoral revision courts whose job it was to compile the registers. The courts made a number of contradictory decisions in different constituencies. We therefore need to know not just how many borough voters were created in 1867–68, but how an experimental, ill-defined, rickety and overloaded system worked thereafter. The Hodgkinson Amendment (see pp. 52–3) proved unworkable, validating all its critics' reservations. New legislation, the Goschen Act (see p. 126), replaced it and restored compounding in 1869. A further Act of considerable practical importance was piloted through the Commons by Charles Dilke in 1878 (see p. 126). Both pieces of legislation increased the number of borough voters well beyond what was intended in 1867. The electorate actually grew by about 40 per cent *between* the second and third Reform Acts and by 26 per cent during the decade 1871–81 alone.

The effects were uneven across the country. Between 1873 and 1882, for example, Plymouth's electorate increased by 191 per cent and that of Swansea by 81 per cent, against population increases in the two boroughs of 8.5 per cent and 24.5 per cent respectively. By contrast, some of the largest boroughs – Leeds, Leicester and Nottingham, for example – though their electorates still increased by about

20 per cent each, saw rises lower than the rate of population growth. In the confusing situation created by the hasty passage of the Disraeli Act, local circumstances were the main determinant of who could vote and who could not. Such determinants included the efficiency of officials, the interpretation of complex rating law and the assiduousness of party agents. The Dilke Act had a significant impact on the size of the electorate in London. The electorate of Chelsea, for example, increased by 33 per cent in five years before the third Reform Act [140].

Such large, uneven and sometimes uncovenanted increases clearly challenge assumptions about the nature of the artisan electorate. It was never so uniformly 'respectable' as some commentators assumed, though it was respectable enough. Important categories were excluded. Those without a one-year residence qualification – which, given inflexible publication dates of registers, could easily stretch to two years – could not vote. Nor could those in receipt of poor relief, which culled a substantial number of the elderly. Nor could adult males living with their parents, unless they had clear separate arrangements for paying rent. Nor could lodgers in rooms whose rent was set at less than £10 a year. Nor could most servants, though the great majority of these were female anyway [148]. The cumulative effect was that slightly fewer than 60 per cent of adult males in the boroughs could vote. Thus, as Davis and Tanner conclude, 'although the late Victorian borough franchise remained exclusive, it was not in any conscious way selective – certainly not in the way that its founders had intended, distinguishing a "respectable" electorate from the "residuum"' [140 p. 327].

The only piece of legislation during Gladstone's first government (1868–74) which focused primarily on electoral reform was the secret ballot for parliamentary elections, introduced in 1872 [Doc. 17 and p. 133]. The ballot question has been under-studied by historians. It appears, of course, as another of the six Chartist 'points' to be ticked off. Yet it raised matters of principle and roused intense passions [Doc. 13]. It is surely significant that the most senior pro-reform Liberal, Lord John Russell, remained an opponent of a secret ballot from 1830 – when it was one of a number of options considered by the Whig reform committee on which he sat – to 1872. In 1871, he informed the Duke of Richmond that he must oppose the ballot 'not only as a change from publicity to secrecy in the performance of a great public duty, but as an obvious prelude to a change from household to universal suffrage' [81 p. 182].

In 1837, the parliamentary radicals, who had gained increased leverage over their Whig allies because Conservative recovery in the election of 1835 left Melbourne's government without a purely Whig majority (see Chapter 3), proposed that the ballot should be introduced as the most desirable item on their continued reform agenda. This horrified the Whig leadership, who regarded the radicals as educated and determined but entirely unrepresentative of popular opinion. Lord Holland called them 'cold and insensible and often as narrow and tyrannical as the worshippers of authority or lovers of power themselves'. The Whigs, of course, had long claimed to speak for the people and to guide them where necessary (see Chapter 2). The secret ballot would deprive these self-appointed people's spokesmen of what they considered a means of legitimate influence. In their eyes, it was an agenda of what Russell called 'clique of democratic reformers' which was 'subversive of liberty' and even 'fatal to all Democratical power'.

The ballot polarised the conflict between 'openness' and corruption. For many senior politicians in the early 1870s as much as in the later 1830s, open declaration of support for one party or another was an honourable, manly business. Secrecy smacked of cowardice. Defenders of open voting also argued that the right to command voters' allegiance was an important part of the structure of paternalism and deference which kept the country loyal and stable [Doc. 14]. For many Conservatives, also, the very fact that open declaration had always been the means of voting was sufficient reason to continue with the practice.

On the other hand, a voter whose political allegiance was open to scrutiny was a voter open to a range of inducements, not all of them legal. The so-called Philosophical Radicals had conducted a long campaign from the 1840s to rid the electoral process of all practices which might render the weak vulnerable to pressure from the strong. Anti-aristocrats like John Bright also argued that Conservative majorities in county seats were buttressed by the open manipulation of landlord control over their tenants. This was proof that the Chandos Amendment (see p. 29) had actually increased corruption. The ballot might, therefore, marginally reduce Conservative strength in the counties but this was not why it became law. Rather, Gladstone became persuaded by Bright that secrecy and the independence which went with it were more appropriate to the enlarged electorate which had been created in 1867–68. It would also dampen the rumbustiousness of the hustings which preceded open elections. The vulgar street theatre elements of electioneering were not to Victorian middle-class taste, though they may have preserved a degree of political interaction between the lower orders (enfranchised or not) and their 'betters'

[Doc. 18]. Their passing seemed in tune with the priorities of a sober age. After 1880, legislation to sustain secret ballots had to be passed annually through parliament, usually without debate. Secret ballots became acknowledged as a permanent feature of the electoral scene only with the Representation of the People Act in 1918 (see Chapter 10 and Appendix I, p. 135).

8 CORRUPTION, REFORM AND REDISTRIBUTION, 1883–85

CORRUPTION

A staggeringly large number of elections in nineteenth-century Britain were corrupt. Increases in the number of voters in 1832 and 1867 did not reduce the number of instances of undue 'influence' – rather the reverse. From the ten general elections held in the years 1832–68, a total of 346 petitions were presented to parliament alleging bribery, and this undoubtedly understated the extent of the problem. As Palmerston, never an overly fastidious politician, told the Commons of his worries: 'I speak it with shame and sorrow, but I verily believe that the extent to which bribery and corruption was carried at the last election, has exceeded anything that has ever been stated within these walls' [20 p. 171]. Perhaps the most notoriously and persistently corrupt borough was St Albans (Hertfordshire) whose six hundred electors were proved to have had at least £38,000 lavished on them in the years 1832–50.

The 1841 general election got the nickname 'the Bribery election', one MP alleging that the 'vast majority' of his colleagues owed their seats in the Commons to 'wholesale corruption' [145 p. 558]. Another MP in 1857 asserted that bribery 'is seen ... in fuller action at this moment than ever before'. Not to be outdone, *The Times* reported: 'The testimony is unanimous that in the General Election of 1865 there was more profuse and corrupt expenditure than was ever known before' [84 p. 28]. Official enquiries revealed that at Lancaster the Liberals and the Conservatives each spent more than £7,000 bribing two-thirds of the town's electorate. Their official returns showed expenditure of less than £1,500 each. Lancaster, though a relatively large borough of 20,000 people, found itself disfranchised for corruption in 1867, alongside Totnes, Reigate and Yarmouth (at 40,000 one of the larger boroughs). The election commissioners dolefully intoned 'the deluge of corruption [in 1865] has been more universal and has reached a higher level of society than ever before' [84 p. 29].

Professor Hanham's researches have revealed that no fewer than 64 English boroughs endured corrupt practice in the form of bribing, treating and other infringements of election law in the years 1865–84 [78 p. 263]. While 35 of these had populations below 20,000 (making identification and subsequent inducements easier to arrange), eight were large boroughs with populations of over 50,000. In some small boroughs it is possible to trace precisely the level of inducement. In the Irish borough of Cashel, for example, 203 electors voted in the 1868 general election. One candidate, Henry Munster bought the allegiance of 25 of the town's 26 butchers by buying their votes at the enormous sum of £30 a head [145 p. 562].

Only after 1867 did concern about corruption lead to concerted pressure for action. It was soon clear that the secret ballot (see pp. 62–3) eliminated neither naked corruption nor influence. In constituencies where electors had been accustomed to 'treating', the Act only increased opportunities to receive bribes from both sides, since where the bribed elector eventually placed his cross would be a secret. Some, however, harboured fears about precisely *how* secret the ballot was, concerns which have never been entirely dispelled in some quarters. More importantly, perhaps, a combination of loyalty and continued fear prevented wholesale changes in voting habits. Most tenants in the counties seemed to have been as loyally Conservative as their landowners and little coercion was necessary. The phrase 'the landed interest' was intended to, and often did, cut across class and status divisions. Similarly, in several industrial boroughs, knowledge of, and loyalty to, a well-established employer was often enough to determine the outcome of an electoral contest. Some historians have referred to 'factory paternalism' as an important form of political influence [64].

The 1880 general election was the most expensive yet fought. Officially, it cost the competing parties £1.7 million but much more was spent by agents, canvassers and other activists than was declared. The true cost certainly exceeded £2 million. On average each candidate declared expenses of £3,128 in the county seats and £1,212 in the boroughs [78 p. 251]. The difference was largely explained by the greater distances county candidates needed to travel to reach their scattered electorates. To these costs should be added outgoings which were considered a perfectly normal part of 'keeping up the interest' in several constituencies: subscriptions to local charities, endowments to worthy local causes and the like. The smaller boroughs saw elections as a welcome opportunity to screw money from eager candidates in order to embellish or provide new amenities for the town. On top of these might be added a range of more dubious inducements. By 1880, assiduous local agents had acquired more than a decade's practice in how to manage larger electorates. Increasingly, they did this by throwing money at the business of influencing voters. Respectability demanded redress. Particularly in the radical and puritanical wing of the Liberal party, the feeling grew that far too much was being spent – even on election items which might be considered legitimate. The sheer cost of elections restricted the range of candidates willing to fight them. Working men could not contemplate being candidates unless they had party and trade union backing. While a lack of working-class candidates was not a major concern for many liberal radicals, deterring the respectable, educated but modestly funded middle classes was a serious issue. The danger existed that parliament would be indefinitely dominated by men of leisure and most of these, at least in the radical characterisation, were idle landowners.

Even among the wealthy themselves, ever mounting cost was a worry since expenditure was threatening to spiral out of control. Specially appointed royal commissions enquired into malpractice in eight boroughs after the 1880 election and their findings shocked MPs [Doc. 21]. In Macclesfield 55 per cent of an electorate of 5,200 took bribes, in Gloucester 38 per cent of 5,760. It was not so much the fact but the extent, and the casual insidiousness, of malpractice which caused alarm. This helped Gladstone to make corrupt practice a cross-party issue when the government announced in January 1881 that legislation would be brought forward to deal with the issue. On the front benches, although detailed questions were raised, there was broad cross-party agreement on the need to limit election expenditure and to define much more precisely what constituted corrupt practice. Some vociferous backbench concerns were raised, especially from Irish MPs, about excessive government interference in electoral freedom and about the danger that decent men might be dissuaded from become candidates. In the parliamentary sessions of 1881 and 1882, preoccupied as they became with Ireland and imperial policy, these were enough to frustrate corrupt practice bills.

It was thus not until 1883 that the Corrupt and Illegal Practices Prevention Act (see p. 133) reached the statute book. The Act restricted each candidate to the employment of only one election agent, whose responsibility it was to make an official return of expenses. It specified for the first time the maximum allowable expenditure for candidates in constituencies of different types. These varied from £200 in the smaller Irish boroughs to £710 for English, Scottish and Welsh counties with 2,000 voters. An extra £40 was allowable for each additional 1,000 voters. These limits were deliberately stringent. Both parties were determined to see the end of days when one candidate could spend £13,000 on a seat, as C. W. W. Wynn had done in fighting – and losing – Montgomeryshire in 1880 [84 p. 156]. The Act also prescribed penalties (which included imprisonment) for those found guilty of corrupt practice.

Gladstone's big stick had the desired effect. Until the First World War, and occasionally thereafter, instances of corrupt practice were unearthed. Worcester was castigated in 1906 for having a persistent hard core of electors prepared to sell their votes for beer or cash. The 1883 Act, however, destroyed the culture of corruption in British elections. The number of petitions alleging corrupt or illegal practice declined from 28 in 1880 to eight in 1885 and five in 1900. The average cost per vote polled (admittedly a very crude indicator because of the likelihood of under-recording before 1883) fell from 18s 9d (94p) in 1880 to approximately 3s 6d (17.5p) in 1910.

REFORM AND REDISTRIBUTION, 1884–85

As early as 1873 Gladstone had considered 'the extension of the Household Suffrage to counties to be [an issue] just & politic in itself, & which cannot long be avoided' [11 p. 263]. With the Conservatives in power from 1874, however, little was heard of the franchise at Westminster before 1880. But it was pursued vigorously enough by organised workers who lived in county, rather than borough, seats, as did most coal miners. In the north-east of England, where many of Britain's biggest pits were concentrated, most miners did not qualify for the vote because their homes, situated for the most part close to the pits in which they worked, lay within the boundaries of the county seats of Northumberland and Durham, rather than the boroughs of Durham City, Morpeth, Sunderland or Newcastle. It is not surprising, therefore, that the north-east was in the forefront of agitation for further franchise changes.

Most working-class reformers in the 1870s shared Gladstone's strong preference for a household, rather than a manhood, suffrage [Doc. 18]. So did rural spokesmen when unionisation belatedly reached some rural workers through Joseph Arch's National Agricultural Labourers' Union. Stereotypical views about a stupid (or at least a gullible) and a drunken rural workforce were widely shared among skilled workers. Here is the Barnsley miner, E. A. Rayner, wondering in 1875 how any 'patriot' could want agricultural labourers to be enfranchised 'when so many are drunken idiots and hardly capable of understanding right from wrong in political matters' [59 p. 291].

Disraeli's unexpected election victory of 1874 changed perspectives. Skilled workers and trade union leaders ruefully reflected, first, that an extended electorate was not as staunchly Gladstonian Liberal as they had assumed and, secondly, that the distribution of seats in 1867 had been cunningly fixed by Disraeli to maximise support for Conservatives in the counties and the smaller boroughs. Some were also reaching the uncomfortable, but significant, conclusion that Liberal political organisations were not keen to promote working men as parliamentary candidates. Two working-class MPs, Alexander MacDonald (representing Stafford) and Thomas Burt (Morpeth), were scant reward for a generation of close political co-operation. The number of working-class candidates standing as Liberals actually declined from 11 in 1874 to six in 1880.

While leader of the opposition in 1877, the Marquis of Hartington had given assurances that the Liberals would be prepared to secure a uniform franchise in boroughs and counties. After the Liberal election victory in 1880, however, Gladstone was in no particular hurry. While a consensus formed that there were few valid arguments against bringing the counties into line with the boroughs, the question of electoral corruption took priority. Gladstone was not ready to consider specific legislation until 1883. Its basic principle would be a large extension of the county franchise. Most Liberals could agree to support this, although the Whig element, from Hartington downwards, was less enthusiastic.

The Conservative response was masterminded by Salisbury, who was now leader of the opposition. As Cranborne in 1867, he had been the sharpest anti-reforming thorn in Disraeli's side (see p. 51). Now he recognised the inevitability of further reform but manoeuvred skilfully to ensure maximum damage limitation for his party. Experience since 1867 had convinced him that Conservatives had little to fear from increasing the number of voters. It was, however, important to have them in the right place. Gladstone's preference had been to deal with county representation as a separate issue before turning to the more complex issue of redistributing seats in a separate session. Salisbury, fearful that the Liberals would call a general election immediately after creating new voters, persuaded the Lords to use its power to reject the Liberal bill. Significantly, a number of Whig peers (fearful for their own positions) supported him. Although, with the Liberals in trouble over Ireland and policy over Egypt, Salisbury would have preferred an immediate general election on the existing franchise, it was not clear how he was to achieve one. So, behind the scenes, he let it be known that he would not oppose a household suffrage in the counties if an agreed policy for the redistribution of seats were to be implemented immediately [80].

To make progress without threatening his own party's fragile unity, Gladstone agreed to the Salisbury strategy. The radical election expert, Charles Dilke, for the Liberals, worked with Salisbury to hammer out cross-party principles for redistribution. Population thresholds were set below which boroughs would be disfranchised and above which extra members would be added. Independent boundary commissioners would do the detailed work constituency by constituency. The consequences are considered below but the passage of both bills went ahead smoothly enough. A unified household franchise and a radical redistribution of seats transformed the political landscape within a few years [79].

CONSEQUENCES

The 1884 Reform Act (see pp. 133–4) is studied less extensively than are either of the earlier franchise changes in 1832 and 1867. This is understandable in one respect, since it did not result from bitter conflict and did not establish new principles. Though some Conservatives, notably Lord Randolph Churchill, had reservations about enfranchising so many rural labourers, it is possible to see 1884 as merely a 'tidying up' exercise with broad cross-party support. Its effects were substantial. It is worth noting that it enfranchised more people than had the earlier Acts, adding about 2.5 million voters – an increase of about 84 per cent. In Ireland the changes were particularly dramatic. The number of voters increased from 230,000 to 737,000 [62]. Many British politicians feared the consequences of so much change to a nation which had become so disaffected. The new voters, it was gloomily assumed, would be predominantly nationalist.

The basis of the franchise after 1884 became the household. More than 80 per cent of voters qualified on this criterion after 1884. However, the wide variety of additional qualifications (including occupation, lodger, university votes and the once ubiquitous forty-shilling freehold) helped to create a significant number of voters entitled to vote in more than one constituency. It has been estimated that these 'pluralists' represented about 7 per cent of the electorate [16; 88]. By the early twentieth century, about half a million voters were pluralists. Many owned property in adjacent constituencies – perhaps in an industrial borough and the county of which it formed part. Some wealthy men might qualify in as many as ten constituencies, though it is doubtful whether they would feel it worth the considerable effort and expense to exercise their rights. Ironically, Joseph Chamberlain, the most charismatic and powerful advocate of democracy in the 1880s – his 'unauthorized programme' of 1885 proposed manhood suffrage and the abolition of plural voting – qualified for six votes.

Redistribution, rather than Disraelian legerdemain, really dished the Whigs. Its long-term effects are complicated by two other developments pulling in the same direction. First, both the political and social supremacy of the landed aristocracy were challenged by the so-called agricultural depression which lasted, on and off, from the 1870s to the end of the century. Politics was an increasingly expensive luxury even for dukes, who were now forced to count the pennies. Secondly, many of the old Whigs opposed Gladstone's Irish policy in 1885–86 and defected to the so-called 'Liberal Unionists'. This proved in some cases to be merely a staging post on the tortured journey towards Salisbury's Conservatives. For a grouping with the strongest possible sense of historical identity and an abiding mission to reform from above, this was a bitter bill to swallow.

Even before Gladstone's Irish grenade was lobbed into the body of his party, however, the portents for Whiggery were not favourable [86]. In the 1860s and 1870s many Whigs had been installed, in effect, as 'second on the ticket' in the two-member constituencies which were the norm in British politics before 1885. Deals and accommodations with Liberal businessmen, professionals and even radicals saw Whigs preserved for the political nation when, forced to fight for a single seat, they would have been cut out [Doc. 23]. The Redistribution Act presented them with exactly this challenge.

By 1885, the Lambton family – the dominant landowning force in County Durham – was feeling the pinch. The Earl of Durham, its head, was trying to engineer a seat for his friend Reginald Brett. Such a task had been effortlessly accomplished many times in the past. Now, however, he confided to Brett: 'I don't like the political outlook. The local manufacturing and coalowning plutocrats mean to divide the county amongst them' [140; 141]. Lambton influence could not win the seat for Brett at the general election. Furthermore, Durham's brother, the Hon. F. W. Lambton, retired from politics in 1885 rather than try to hang on to his South Durham constituency.

These were not isolated examples. At the 1885 general election, 105 Liberal MPs who could be described as great landowners or relatives and clients of the aristocracy were returned. This represented 31.4 per cent of the Liberal complement in the House of Commons. In the elections of 1874 and 1880 (one lost and one won), the proportion had been remarkably stable at 43 per cent. The old Whig connection, the most successful and long-lived combination of the last two centuries, was almost played out. No fewer than 321 MPs sitting in parliament at the dissolution in 1885 did not return to the new House. Of these 186 were Liberals: 83 chose to retire and no fewer than 85 were defeated in an election – be it remembered – which the Liberals won comfortably overall. The 'new' Liberals of 1885 were disproportionately journalists, intellectuals, lawyers and doctors. The flickering torch of Liberalism was being passed from a landowning elite to the professionals and experts. It would not make them regularly electable [*Doc. 22*].

Salisbury's insistence that Redistribution must accompany reform demonstrated considerable tactical acumen. It ensured that vital bridgehead in the boroughs of southern England upon which Conservative strength would rest right through the twentieth century. He had alerted Beaconsfield (the title Disraeli took when elevated to the peerage in 1876) to the long-term possibilities after the election defeat of 1880. He now negotiated hard with Dilke to secure what he wanted. A majority of the 132 small boroughs released for redistribution in 1885 (see p. 134) had been in Liberal hands. Their transfer to the counties and newly created suburban boroughs boosted the Conservatives, especially around London. The number of MPs for what might be called 'Greater London' increased from 22 MPs to 62 – still a gross under-representation in terms of population but a substantial advance nevertheless. In 1885, the Conservatives won 36 of these seats [17].

Many of the new single-member borough constituencies were carved out of the more populous, and increasingly prosperous, parts of counties. This too benefited the Conservatives. The suburban middle classes valued their hard-won property and did not favour gratuitous disturbance. They had never been much charmed by radicals and a Liberal party in which Chamberlain, Dilke and Bright all held positions of influence did not appeal. Nor, within a year or so, would they prove any keener on Mr Gladstone's latest big idea – Home Rule for Ireland. The suburban voter became predominantly a Tory voter. Salisbury's insight into the psychology of a social group for whom he privately expressed complete contempt provided what was probably the biggest single boost his party ever received. The electoral hegemony of the Conservative party in the years 1886–1997 owed more to the shrewd cynicism of the Marquess of Salisbury than it did to the meretricious chicanery of the Earl of Beaconsfield.

Finally, did the changes of 1884 bring about the much-delayed emergence of democracy in Britain? Contemporaries were anxious to allege that it did. Joseph Chamberlain's *Radical Programme* of 1885 – aimed squarely at the new rural voters – contained the following Preface: 'government of the people by the people ... has at last been effectively secured' [148 *p. 724*]. Sir Henry Maine's influential book, *Popular Government*, suggested in 1886 that the third Reform Act had created 'unmoderated democracy'.

It was not so. A household, not a manhood, suffrage had been created. The total number of electors entitled to vote in 1885 was 5.7 million. The combined exertions of local party agents, economic growth and rising living standards increased the number to 7.7 million by the time of the election of December 1910, the last before the First World War. The best estimates suggest that this represented only between two-fifths and two-thirds of the adult male population of the United Kingdom. The categories excluded in 1867 (see Chapter 7) remained so after 1884–85. The list is long. It included sons living in their parents' homes, live-in servants, recipients of poor relief (including from 1906 those parents who claimed free school meals for their children) and aliens (an important category after the widespread Jewish immigration of the 1880s and 1890s). The most numerous absentees, however, were those who might have been entitled to register but who, for a variety of reasons, never did. Many casual and unskilled workers never lived in a fixed abode long enough to register. Of those who did, the effort to get on to a 'list', which many believed only gave the authorities a means of 'checking up' on them, was not worth the paltry reward of voting for a political party.

Such men lived disproportionately in the larger cities. It is not surprising, therefore, that the proportion of adult males with the vote differed substantially from constituency to constituency. Three-quarters of Oxford's adult male population could vote in the early twentieth century; in the east-end London constituency of Bethnal Green barely two-fifths could [17 *p. 8*]. Counties overall had a larger proportion of registered voters than did boroughs and more adult Englishmen voted than did adult Scotsmen.

Little note is taken of the significance of this 'submerged third' of adult male non-voters. In one sense, this is understandable. Attention from the last decade of the nineteenth century was insistently focused on votes for women (see Chapter 9). The old 'respectability' arguments tied up with the household suffrage rapidly became submerged. Furthermore, it helped the women's propaganda campaign to let it be assumed that even the lowest and most reprehensible of men could vote in parliamentary elections while the highest and most worthy women could not. This muddied the waters still further. What the

Victorians called the 'residuum' had few to champion their political rights.

The misleading assumptions of Chamberlain and Maine (see p. 73) have been widely accepted. Probably (and allowing for the inevitable difficulties of categorisation at the margin) 40 per cent of the electorate was middle class whereas only 20 per cent of jobs – at most – could be so categorised. We should be very suspicious of claims that the Reform Acts of 1867–68 and 1884 created an electorate dominated by the working class. According to Pelling, only 95 constituencies were so at the turn of the century [87 pp. 419–20]. The irony is that the nation which liked to call itself the 'cradle of democracy' possessed on the eve of the First World War one of the most restrictive franchises in western Europe.

PART FOUR: VOTES FOR WOMEN – AND MANY MORE MEN

9 THE WOMEN'S SUFFRAGE CAMPAIGN, 1867–1914

IMAGES AND STEREOTYPES

The public image of the 'votes for women' campaign is a militant one. The activities of the Women's Social and Political Union (WSPU) from 1903 were designed to win maximum publicity. The 'argument of the broken window pane', storming the House of Commons, hunger strikes, and finally the desperate act of martyrdom by Emily Davidson in throwing herself under the King's horse during the running of the Derby in 1913 all achieved that [120]. The unwise responses of Asquith's Liberal government – force-feeding of hunger strikers and the infamous 'Cat and Mouse' Act which saw suffragettes released from prison and then promptly rearrested – were counter-productive in gaining support even among sceptical voters for the women's cause.

Yet the suffragettes did not succeed before 1914 and it is doubtful how much their campaigns achieved, if anything [87; 95; 108]. *The Manchester Guardian* referred to their 'diseased emotionalism'. The suffragettes divided women. In 1906 *Punch* published a famous cartoon, 'The 'Shrieking Sister', which shows a 'sensible woman' berating a suffragette. The caption reads: '*YOU* help our cause? Why, you're its worst enemy!' There is plenty of evidence that this was not mere anti-feminist propaganda. Divisions over tactics were costly. Membership of the National Union of Women's Suffrage Societies (NUWSS), founded in 1897, grew rapidly after 1903 in response to the WSPU. It had more than 50,000 members by 1914, many of whom favoured moral force over militancy. The 'Women's Freedom League' was founded in 1907 by the socialist Charlotte Despard and other ILP (Independent Labour Party) sympathisers such as Anne Sanderson and Teresa Billington Greig. It recognised the importance of militancy but attacked the attention-seeking antics of the WSPU, the excessive personalisation of issues around the Pankhursts and their apparent willingness to 'sell out' over a restricted female franchise. Some acidly noted that this upper-middle-class family could afford to indulge itself in shouting down ministers and interrupting the royal mail, heedless of the fact that their working-class supporters might be harmed by the angry reactions of employers.

The public image of violence, which derives overwhelmingly from the last decade before the First World War, misses much which is important about the women's suffrage campaign. First, the cause of female enfranchisement had been advanced long before the suffragette campaigns of the Edwardian period. The most famous early statement was *A Vindication of the Rights of Woman*, written by Mary Wollstonecraft in 1792 as the deliberate counterpart to Tom Paine's *Rights of Man* [*Doc. 1*] (see p. 12 and Chronology). Recent research has also revealed the extent of women's involvement in the Chartist movement of the 1830s and 1840s [60; 117]. The so-called 'Kensington Society' of middle-class, educated women organised a petition in 1866 signed by 1,499 women calling for a household suffrage for both men and women. The first developed argument heard in the House of Commons was presented by John Stuart Mill during debates on the Second Reform Bill in 1867 [*Doc. 12*]. A National Society for Women's Suffrage (NSWS) was established in 1867. Thereafter, the question remained more or less permanently, though rarely prominently, on the Westminster agenda. The role of John Bright's brother, Jacob, Liberal MP for Manchester and a successful businessman there, was significant here. His initiative enfranchised women ratepayers in 1869 (see p. 77) and he also piloted the Married Woman's Property Act on to the statute book in 1870. In addition, he introduced woman's franchise bills into parliament regularly throughout the 1870s [86 *p. 230*].

In 1884, the National Liberal Federation passed a motion supporting female enfranchisement at its Conference in Leeds. When the pottery businessman William Woodall, MP for his home town of Stoke-on-Trent, raised the question during debates on the third Reform Act (see pp. 70–1), 137 members supported him [80 *p. 6*] with 271 against. As the male franchise expanded, so the logical case for admitting women grew. If the intention remained to enfranchise respectable folk, women argued, where was the logic in giving agricultural labourers the vote in 1884 when their employers, who might be widowed tenant farmers, could not vote?

The women's suffrage campaign failed to thrive in the second half of the nineteenth century for a number of reasons. Dominant cultural assumptions in the Victorian age revolved around 'separate spheres' or the notion of 'the Angel in the House' [97; 101]. On this construction, men were concerned with action, employment and the intellectual and political spheres while women should be revered for more gentle, caring qualities. Their essentially 'emotional', 'unreflective' and 'sentimental' natures made them ideal home-makers and mothers. Some went further. Women who tried to divide the time between home management and campaigns for the vote were branded as inadequates, or even unhinged. That women should prefer a career to marriage was almost, of itself, proof of unworthiness to enjoy the full benefits of citizenship [Doc. 26]. The logical conclusion from premises such as this was that society worked more harmoniously if men and women respected each other's God-given space: men the public and women the private.

Broadly speaking, this was the view taken by William Gladstone, prime minister at the time of Woodall's proposal in 1884. His opposition had been sufficient to switch the allegiance of many Liberal MPs who were in principle in favour of votes for women. When the issue surfaced again in 1892, Gladstone responded in characteristic fashion by writing a pamphlet, *Female Suffrage*, in which he dilated on the likely effects of a woman's franchise. Asserting that women were 'generally indifferent' to the vote anyway, he argued that their having it would effect 'a fundamental change in the whole social function of women. ... The fear I have is, lest we should invite her unwittingly to trespass upon the delicacy, the purity, the refinement, the elevation of her own nature, which are the present sources of its power' [114 p. 11]. Such orotund opacity was characteristic of Gladstone's discourse but his assumption that women already had sufficient power through their dominance within the private sphere was clear enough. It was widely shared.

WOMEN AND LOCAL POLITICS

Many sceptics about women's suffrage in the 1880s also pointed out that women already had the franchise in many areas of public life which, if not exactly personal, might be considered literally closer to the world of home and hearth. Women ratepayers could vote for poor law guardians under the terms of the Poor Law Amendment Act of 1834. The Municipal Franchise Act of 1869 permitted women ratepayers to vote on the same terms as men, though this was restricted to unmarried women three years later [98 p. 7] (see Chronology). They could not only vote for school boards after their creation under the Education Act of 1870 but could also be elected to those boards. The County Councils Act of 1888, which followed the third Reform Act, also gave women householders the vote. The Parish and Rural District

Councils Act of 1894 permitted them both to vote and to stand as candidates. By 1900, about one million unmarried ratepaying women qualified for the vote in local elections. By no means all were middle class, as was the widespread assumption both at the time and among historians until recently [98 *p. 32*]. John Burns, an ex-engineer, trade unionist and Labour politician in London who later joined the Liberal party, passed legislation in 1907 permitting women to stand as candidates in both borough and county council elections.

Male supporters of a woman's franchise, such as William Woodall, Burns and David Lloyd George, noted that women had exercised the local vote sensibly. Their record as local representatives on district councils, school boards and the like had generally been exemplary. As Burns pointed out in 1907, 'In regard to disorderly houses, and in many questions of public health administration, women were better suited than men, in many cases they were the only persons qualified to carry out the work' [98 *p. 46*]. Opponents turned these arguments around by suggesting that such service only confirmed that separate spheres *did* exist and that women were best kept away from central politics. Supporters responded by pointing out how much legislation in Edwardian England was concerned with home and family. As Ethel Snowden, the suffrage campaigner who was also the wife of the Labour pacifist politician Philip Snowden, put it in her book, *The Feminist Movement* (1913): 'because the special sphere of woman is the home, women ought to have the vote' [18 *p. 208*].

The dominant suffragist argument was that women deserved the vote on the same terms as men. The changes of 1867–68 and 1884 produced, in effect, a household suffrage (see p. 73). Such a qualification would result in a franchise skewed towards spinsters and widows. This grated with many MPs. They had assimilated the 'separate spheres' argument and argued that women were not 'proper' examples of their sex unless they had fulfilled their manifest destiny to marry. Also, why should the house-owning brothel madam have the vote when the respectable wife was denied it [17]? Such reasoning ignored the uncomfortable fact of demographic change. The birth rate slowed perceptibly from 30.2 per 1,000 in the 1890s to 27.5 in the 1900s. Since infant mortality was always higher among males than females, one important consequence of this change was that the proportion of unmarried women in the population began to increase. In 1891, 281 women out of every 1,000 over 19 years of age were unmarried; by 1911 this had increased to 302 [96 *p. 135*]. More perfectly respectable women were unable to fulfil their 'manifest destiny' of marriage – a trend which would be accentuated by the ravages of the First World War.

THE LIBERAL AND LABOUR PARTIES

There was also an important tactical consideration. Most supporters of women's suffrage within parliament were Liberals and radicals. After 1893, suffragists in the north of England established strong links with the Independent Labour Party (ILP). After 1900, many members of the Labour Representation Committee (LRC, but officially renamed the Labour party in 1906) were also supporters [93; 109; 111]. Most Conservative backbenchers were strongly hostile. The evidence from Liberal election agents in the constituencies, and inferences drawn from general election results in the 1880s and 1890s, suggested that women property owners would be predominantly Conservative supporters. This impression was strengthened by the work of women party activists and by the extent of the support women gave to the Conservative Primrose League. In the 1890s, half a million League members were women.

Left-wing politicians, therefore, had to balance their support for the idea of women voters against the likely political consequences. If giving women the vote would strengthen an already alarming Conservative electoral dominance in the late 1880s and 1890s, perhaps it was better to concentrate on other single-issue campaigns, such as the disestablishment of the established churches, secular education or temperance reform. The Liberal split over Ireland in 1886 did the women's cause no favours. The radicals who accompanied Chamberlain into 'Liberal Unionism' were, in general, keener on 'gas and water socialism' than on votes for women. No franchise bill was debated in the House of Commons in the years 1886–92. One historian suggests that 'the period from 1884 to 1897 marked the nadir of the women's suffrage movement in Britain' [114 *p. 12*].

On the other hand, the likely effects of a woman householder franchise enabled Conservative leaders to offer mild support for the cause. The Marquess of Salisbury was almost certainly hostile in principle. As Cranborne, he had been a fierce opponent of Disraeli in 1867 (see p. 51) but he was too acute to pass up a tactical opportunity. He thus suggested that the influence of women would 'weigh in a direction which, in an age so material as ours, is exceedingly valuable – namely in the direction of morality and religion' [90 *p. 9*]. Salisbury's immediate successors, Balfour and Bonar Law, were keener on the idea of a safe, propertied electorate including women as well as men. Among the ranks of pro-women's suffrage Conservative backbenchers were Algernon Borthwick and Sir Albert Rollit. They remained heavily outnumbered by opponents right down to the First World War. In the debate on the Representation of the People Bill in 1913, for example, only 28 Conservatives supported the motion with 140 against. The Liberal members, by contrast, split almost two to one in favour [88 p. 188].

In some ways, the biggest disappointment for suffragists was the lack of wholehearted commitment from the Labour party. Of the three political parties after 1900, Labour was the most sympathetic to the women's cause. However, the relationship between suffrage supporters and the party was not an easy one. After early co-operation with the ILP in the 1890s, women frequently found themselves rebuffed by Labour supporters who gave greater priority to enfranchising all 'adults'. In the definitional sense, adults obviously came in two sexes. However, women accused Labour politicians of a fudge which implied priority for adult males. In any case, the suffrage for all adults commanded little support in either house of parliament. The majority view within the suffrage movement also was that universal suffrage was an impractical goal. Therefore, women should agitate for a more restrictive franchise which included them. The Pankhursts also wanted to coerce a partial, propertied women's franchise from the legislature: 'The Women's Social and Political Union are *not* asking for a vote for every woman, but simply that sex shall cease to be a disqualification for the franchise' [18 p. 215].

Before 1914, of course, the Labour party had no prospect of power. The 42 MPs elected in 1910, its maximum pre-war complement, were only half the number of the Irish nationalists, who could exert greater leverage on the Liberal party. Labour politicians in local government were even less committed to votes for women than were their Westminster counterparts. Activists in Wolverhampton were voicing a typical view when they urged in 1902 that Labour should give priority to adult *male* suffrage [83]. Virtually all trade unions were dominated by men. The Lancashire cotton textile unions, which included a large woman membership, stood almost alone [99; 105; 108].

Trade unionists, particularly in the heavy industries, were strong believers in separate spheres – with tea ready on the table when the working man came home. Mine workers, the most heavily unionised group, operated within a strongly accentuated male culture. The miners did not defect from the Liberals to support for the Labour party until 1909 but those trade unions which had supported Labour from the beginning were scarcely more sympathetic to women's suffrage. 'Time and again local Labour politicians [in the years before the First World War] appealed to an explicitly male audience – an audience of "breadwinners", of respectable family men, who were determined to assert their rights and proclaim their independence' [83 p. 158]. Bruce Glasier, Chairman of the ILP, told the organisation in 1903 that women could rely on Labour MPs (once elected in sufficient numbers) to represent the interests of women as effectively as those of men. The suffrage response was predictable [Doc. 24]. The newly founded WSPU of the Pankhursts quickly broke with the Labour party and embraced those militant tactics which attracted publicity and odium in more or less equal measure. They perplexed Lloyd George, perhaps their staunchest supporter in government after 1905. He wondered why they wasted their energies attacking him when there were so many genuine opponents on whom to concentrate their fire.

TURNING THE TIDE?

The suffrage movement made sufficient headway to win a succession of votes in the House of Commons on resolutions introduced by backbenchers. Every year from 1908–11, private members' bills received healthy majorities which revealed a substantial cross-section of support. The bill introduced by the Labour MP David Shackleton in 1910 had a majority of 110: 161 Liberals, 31 Labour, 20 Irish Nationalists and as many as 87 Conservative–Unionists supported it [4 p. 152]. This, however, was less than half the battle. It was necessary to persuade the Liberal government to grant sufficient parliamentary time to give a woman's franchise bill chance to become law [151]. That was difficult, since it was not an issue on which the party could agree. The prime minister, Herbert Asquith, was opposed. Furthermore, after the two general elections of 1910, the Liberals had lost their majority in the House of Commons and needed support from minority parties, particularly the Irish Nationalists, to survive. The Nationalists, while not opposed in principle, increasingly took the view that a contentious bill on women's suffrage would drain vital parliamentary time away from their own great cause of Home Rule. This consideration explains why, after a number of Commons successes, the 1912 'Conciliation Bill' was defeated. The other immense stumbling block was the House of Lords. This body was controlled by hereditary peers and it was a cardinal principle of hereditary succession that men took precedence over older women. A majority there seemed highly unlikely.

The increasing climate of violence, which included trade union as well as feminist militancy, persuaded Asquith to take action in 1912. His Franchise and Redistribution Act shrewdly returned to the problem of the 40 per cent of men who remained without the vote. His proposal was to increase the number of male voters by up to three million. The calculation was that such a large jump would reveal the women's position to be so anomalous that it would be far less contentious to slip in clauses which enfranchised 'safe', propertied, women. The Conservatives, already smarting from government tactics over the House of Lords the previous year (see pp. 85–6), refused to co-operate. Their pressure was instrumental in persuading the Speaker of the Commons to make an important procedural ruling in 1913 [111]. He announced that any amendments involving women's franchise would so transform the intention of the original bill that it would have to be withdrawn and re-presented. All the time so far taken was thus wasted. The suffrage campaign seemed to be back to square one. The militancy of 1913 was on an unprecedented scale but it was probably counter-productive. It certainly provoked the same arguments about embittered women who traduced their sex [*Doc. 27*].

In 1914, the First World War brought all domestic skirmishings to a shuddering halt. It also transformed the attitude of the suffragettes. Now the reviled Pankhursts, staunch patriots, found themselves speaking for majority opinion. Suffragettes were released from prison and Emmeline Pankhurst sent out a circular to all WSPU members: 'It is obvious that even the most vigorous militancy of the W.S.P.U. is for the time being rendered less effective by the contrast with the infinitely greater violence done in the present war not to mere property and economic prosperity alone, but to human life' [114 *p. 248*]. Feeling in the NUWSS was more ambivalent, especially in the early stages of the war. Some attended peace meetings and individual suffragists were associated with the movement for a negotiated peace. However, most women quickly realised the political dangers. In Lord Robert Cecil's words: 'Action of that kind [peace agitation] will undoubtedly make it very difficult for the friends of Woman Suffrage in both the Unionist and Ministerialist parties' [88 *p. 138*]. Suffragists and suffragettes alike bent their shoulders to winning the war [*Doc. 28*].

10 TOWARDS DEMOCRACY, 1910–18

THE HOUSE OF LORDS

Votes for women was not the only major issue concerning representation which provoked high controversy in the Edwardian age. A reformist Liberal government quickly came into conflict with the House of Lords [4; 6; 18]. The Lords contained an inbuilt Conservative majority throughout the nineteenth century but this had increased substantially after the Irish Home Rule conflict caused so many Whig peers to join the 'Conservative and Unionist Party'. On the Irish issue, home rulers in the Lords could be outvoted by at least ten to one.

For most of the preceding century this imbalance had created few difficulties. Grey had extracted a reluctant promise from William IV to create sufficient peers to pass the Great Reform Act (see p. 25) but the Lords capitulated in time. In 1860, the upper house had rejected Gladstone's paper duties bill but they passed his budget the following year, into which the paper duties had been neatly folded. During the years of Conservative dominance from 1886 to 1905, the government's wishes were dutifully done. In the years 1886–92 and 1895–1902, of course, the prime minister, Salisbury, headed one of the most senior aristocratic families in the land. Britain does not have a written constitution, so there was nothing which the Lords could not, in theory, endorse or reject. However, a workable convention had developed during the nineteenth century. Peers endorsed finance legislation passed by the elected House more or less automatically and might pass amendments to other legislation reaching them from the Commons. It claimed the right to reject outright only legislation concerned with fundamental constitutional change.

This convention broke under the strains imposed on it by the Liberal government's policies from 1906. In 1906, the peers rejected a Liberal education bill which would have ended denominational religious instruction in state schools. They also rejected the government's plans to end plural voting. The Liberals pointed out that no fewer than

17 different qualifications governed the right to vote. It was in principle wrong to allow the inevitably richer minority opportunity to vote in different constituencies. The Lords, who knew that plural voters were overwhelmingly Conservatives, responded that they felt justified in rejecting this constitutional proposal, not least since Ireland (where Conservatives and Unionists were relatively weak) was so heavily over-represented in terms of its population. The Lords also rejected compulsory land valuation and liquor licensing proposals.

These rejections, though they made Liberal supporters seethe, did not provoke an immediate government response, despite the fact that the Liberals had received one of the biggest electoral mandates in history at the general election of 1906. The crisis came soon after Asquith succeeded Campbell-Bannerman as prime minister in 1908. In consequence, David Lloyd George was promoted to the Chancellorship of the Exchequer. Lloyd George introduced his so-called 'People's Budget' the following year. The rising star of the Liberal party, 'LG' had already earned a reputation as a baiter of the aristocracy. His Welsh nonconformist origins and under-privileged background made land reform (whose target was clearly inherited wealth) his particular hobby-horse. However, there is little to suggest that Lloyd George introduced his Budget with the express purpose of inducing the Lords to reject it, and thus catapult Britain into its biggest constitutional crisis since 1832. Had this been the intention, then the much more emollient Asquith would have stopped him.

The Budget was framed to assist mainstream Liberal policy. The government sought £16 million to pay for its naval rearmament programme and the new old-age pensions, which were initially funded by the taxpayer, not by compulsory insurance as later. The government was also determined to preserve free trade and fight off the Conservatives' preference for tariff reform. The most effective way to do this was to raise taxation. Lloyd George believed that the Lords would follow precedent and allow the finance bill to pass, however strong their reservations. His Budget was, however, loaded with items expressly designed to isolate the Lords and, perhaps, to pay them back for rejection of so much significant earlier legislation. Lloyd George proposed a 20 per cent tax on the unearned increment in land values, a 10 per cent tax on any benefits which lessors might enjoy at the end of a lease and a tax on undeveloped land [18 *p. 180*). These taxes would bring in very little but their populist purpose was clear. They targeted a privileged group for whom Lloyd George had little time while offering the possibility of a party political fight in the guise of 'peers versus people'.

The Lords rejected the Budget by 350 votes to 75 in November 1909. The rejection was not a fit of pique but a considered strategy agreed upon by Arthur Balfour, the Conservative leader and Lord Lansdowne, the party leader in the Lords. Some have seen it as 'insane' defiance of the wishes of a government with a huge parliamentary majority. It was almost bound to lead to legislative wing-clipping. However, it was defensible in party-political terms. The Conservative position was that the Budget was a political contrivance which had smuggled in proposals designed to set class against class. The Lords were entitled to reject it since they claimed that it was only in part a finance bill. The electorate should have the opportunity of pronouncing upon it before the Lords would let it pass. Precipitating a general election could be good politics. The Liberals had recently lost some important by-elections. The Conservatives were almost bound to emerge with more MPs in the Commons; they might even win. In such a case, no more would be heard of House of Lords reform and a great deal more of the Liberal *bête noire*, tariff reform.

The Conservatives did not win but they ran the Liberals very close. Lloyd George's anti-aristocratic harangues about the illegitimate power of 'five hundred men, ordinary men chosen accidentally from among the unemployed' [89 *p. 125*] went down like a lead balloon in southern England, where the Liberals lost heavily. Deference and loyalty to ancient authority still counted for much in the shires. The Liberals could continue in government, but only with the support of the Irish Nationalists and, if necessary, the Labour party. Neither of these groups, however, was likely to support the Conservatives against constitutional reform.

Asquith thus introduced a parliament bill [*Doc. 25*] in April 1910 but progress on a highly delicate constitutional matter was slow, not least because Edward VII died the following month and the government did not wish to expose his inexperienced son, George V, to constitutional embarrassment before he had played himself into his new role. A Constitutional Conference, designed to get cross-party agreement, meandered on during the summer and autumn, before falling apart. George V was put in the same position as William IV in 1832 when his prime minister – Earl Grey – had asked him to create sufficient peers to pass the Parliament Bill if the Lords remained intransigent. George now agreed on two conditions: the Liberals must seek yet another mandate from the electorate and his agreement over new peers must remain secret during the election campaign.

The second election of 1910, reluctantly fought during the Christmas shopping season, produced an almost identical outcome. The

Parliament Bill duly reappeared and the Lords were now faced with a stark choice: either accept restriction on their legislative powers or heavy dilution of their membership and the same outcome a few months later. The choice was not difficult. Although plenty of 'last-ditchers' refused to be browbeaten, official Conservative opposition was dropped. The Lords passed the Parliament Bill by 131 votes to 114. The majority actually included 37 Conservatives who, led by Lord Curzon, preferred honourable retreat to any dilution of blue blood. For the minority, Lord Willoughby de Broke accused the Liberals of 'making war on the constitution of this country' and of seeking to break the Lords now in order to push through a hated Home Rule Bill for Ireland soon afterwards [4 *p. 191*].

Were the Liberals 'making war on the constitution'? The historian, at a safe distance from these highly charged events, is more likely to conclude that they had missed an important opportunity. They had clarified that the Lords could not tamper with finance legislation and could only delay other legislation for two years or so. They had also taken the opportunity to reduce the length of parliament from seven years to five – not necessarily a helpful move for a radical government bent on controversial legislation. But much more could have been done. Notice the preamble to the Parliament Act [*Doc. 25*] which promised proposals for a more representative second chamber. Nothing was subsequently heard of these. Some Liberals had specific proposals, but no consensus existed. Others would have preferred, simply and cleanly, to abolish the Lords. This would have left parliament without a chamber having the useful function of scrutinising contentious legislation and improving it after detailed discussion. The Liberals also had other important social and diplomatic issues which took priority. The limited changes brought about by the Parliament Act (see p. 134) had taken the best part of two gruelling years to effect. It is easy to understand why it seemed easier to let the matter of radical reconstruction drop. The Lords thus remained without their veto but with their essentially accidental composition unsullied. They were also keen to use the delaying powers which remained to them. These proved crucial. In 1913, they refused to endorse the government's proposals for Irish Home Rule and for Church of England disestablishment in Wales. Liberal bills to end the practice of plural voting were rejected twice – in July 1913 and one year later, ten days before the outbreak of war. The prospect of carrying these contentious measures was ended by the outbreak of war. The upper house thus retained substantial negative powers on the wobbly warrant of accident of birth. The problem of a second chamber dominated by the principle of hereditary succession remained unresolved for more than 80 years.

WAR AND THE FRANCHISE

The outbreak of war, it seemed, had blunted the Liberals' reforming impulse. Yet the war proved to be the crucial accelerator of franchise reform. Lloyd George toyed with refusing Asquith's offer of promotion to the War Office in any Cabinet in July 1916 and drafted a letter to him citing the franchise question as the reason:

> I have taken a strong line in Cabinet on the question of the enfranchisement of our soldiers. I feel they have a right to a voice in choosing the Government that sends them to face peril and death. Were I now to accept a new office in the Government it would fetter my action when the Cabinet came to decide that great issue as they must soon. [88 p. 51].

Patriotism was also the key to Conservative movement on the issue. The pitiable sacrifices of human life on the Western Front, both among the ordinary soldiery and in the officer class, induced a sense of shared loss. Several MPs saw active service in France and had reason to reflect that the nice calculations about 'respectability' and 'safety' which had contrived to keep almost 40 per cent of adult males off the electoral roll now seemed petty and unworthy. It was largely as a result of Conservative pressure that a Speaker's Conference was established in 1916 to achieve cross-party support for electoral reform. Consensus rapidly formed around proposals for universal manhood suffrage [88]. Women's massive contribution to the war effort [Doc. 30] also finally convinced many doubters of the justice of their cause. The Speaker's Conference, however, was not prepared to recommend votes for women on the same basis as men. It was rapidly agreed that votes for women could only be sold to parliament if the great majority of female voters were married, mature and could be linked in some way to the old household qualification, either directly or through their husbands. Lively debate ensued on whether the appropriate age of female discretion should be 35 or 30 [Doc. 29]. Without a clear recommendation from the Conference, the coalition government opted for the lower threshold.

When the Conference's recommendations appeared as draft legislation in 1917, they shocked the Conservative party, especially in the grassroots. It believed (quite wrongly as things turned out) that such a large increase in the number of voters would work against its interests.

Conservative representatives on the Speaker's Conference were excitedly denounced as 'traitors' as 259 local parties rejected its recommendations, while only 32 endorsed them [88; 93; 112]. The party realised that, in the climate of wartime sacrifice, it could not oppose the principle of universal manhood suffrage without losing credibility. Exploiting the government's desire to maintain consensus on voting rights, it did, however, work extremely successfully to change the detail in the proposed legislation in its favour.

The Speaker's Conference had recommended proportional representation, though of different types, to ensure a fairer voting system. The Conservative majority in the Lords favoured this idea. Tory peers believed that proportional representation would put an end to the dangerous nonsense of a radical government bent on change being elected with a large majority by misguided voters – as it considered had happened in 1906. Both the party leadership in the Commons and the rank and file thought proportional representation newfangled, fiddly and difficult for what would be substantially a new and unsophisticated electorate to understand. Out went PR – except for the seven university seats where, it was assumed, voters would be educated enough to use it wittingly. The decision on proportional representation almost certainly contributed to the dominance of the Conservative party in British politics over the next 80 years.

Redistribution of seats and plural voting were also prime Conservative targets. The party succeeded in getting substantial change in the distribution of Irish seats. While it could not reduce their number, redistribution favoured the Protestant–Unionist interest. Elsewhere, the boundary commissioners' statutory work of equalising constituency sizes favoured areas where the party had done well since the 1880s and where the bedrock of their support would remain throughout the twentieth century. An extension in the number of suburban seats, especially in the south-east, worked in the Conservatives' favour, as did redistribution which further reduced the degree of urban and commercial 'penetration' in rural seats. Overall, redistribution alone probably helped the party win 30 more seats, almost all of which would otherwise have been Liberal. On one calculation, the number of seats dominated by a middle-class electorate increased from 48 to almost 200 in 1918.

The Speaker's Conference had been determined to take an axe to the complexities of plural voting. Plural voters numbered approximately half a million, were mostly financially comfortable and all agreed that they were predominantly Tory in sympathy. The Conservatives acquiesced in the reduction of numbers to about 159,000 who qualified on business premises and about 68,000 university graduates [88]. They did, however, extract an important concession. Businessmen in a large town could now vote as individuals in one constituency of that town and could use their business vote in another constituency in the same town. This ensured, first, that many more business voters were created and, secondly, that the business vote was more widely used than before. Both developments helped swing a significant number of marginal seats into the Tory camp until plural voting was finally abolished by a Labour government in 1948 (see Chronology).

REFORM AND PARTY POLITICS

A lively debate has developed about the party political implications of the Representation of the People Act (see p. 135). One contribution [148 *pp. 736–7*] argued that it was 'of first importance in Labour's replacing the Liberal party as the principal party of progress. ... The growth of the Labour Party before 1914 was limited not by "natural" social and political restrictions, but artificially by the "franchise and registration system that excluded the greater part of its likely support".' Others who examined the registration and sociological data have suggested that the Act should not be given special prominence. Geoffrey Searle, for example, notes that Labour made equal progress in local government elections during the years immediately following the First World War, despite the fact that these continued to be conducted on the more restrictive householder and lodger franchise. He also suggests that the proportion of working-class voters increased only from 76 per cent to 80 per cent after the Act. It is often overlooked that the old system excluded a significant number of lower-middle-class voters, particularly young men who lived in furnished rented accommodation. He concludes that 'If Labour benefited from the new electoral system at all, this, it seems, was mainly because of the changes made to constituency boundaries' [119 *pp. 148–9*].

The creation of more mining constituencies strengthened Labour in what was to become its political heartland. The number of seats in which miners comprised 30 per cent of the electorate or more increased from 35 to 55 in 1918 [93; 150]. The party's major reorganisation under Arthur Henderson in 1917–18 also equipped it to profit both from the Liberal party's split into 'Asquith' and 'Lloyd George' Liberals, and also from Lloyd George's effective 'imprisonment' by a Conservative-dominated coalition after the 1918 general election. The substantial growth in trade union membership also provided the party with funds to fight elections based on a suffrage which was not so far short of universal. The Conservatives, meanwhile, did well out of the extensive electoral redistribution which increased the number of suburban seats, especially in the home counties. Kent, Surrey, Middlesex and Essex combined had only 15 seats before the 1918 redistribution, but 40 afterwards. The parties found themselves appealing to what was overwhelmingly a new electorate. About three-quarters of those who participated in the general election of December 1918 were voting in a parliamentary election for the first time. Apart from the married women who dominated the female vote, most were young men. Many of these had been debarred from voting before by the restrictive, and strictly enforced, lodger qualifications or had been living with their parents.

The Representation of the People Act of 1918 (see p. 135) did not produce universal suffrage. Apart from the substantial minority of still unenfranchised women, between 5 and 7 per cent of adult males were not registered to vote for one reason or another in the early 1920s. Still, the Act radically altered politics in Britain. A few leading politicians still found it difficult to get their heads around the idea of women voters. Herbert Asquith was one such. In a private letter from 1920 he described women as 'hopelessly ignorant of politics, credulous to the last degree, and flickering with gusts of sentiment like a candle in the wind' [119 *p. 149*]. They had, of course, overwhelmingly rejected the dubious blandishments of the Asquith wing of the Liberal party, which won only 28 seats and 1.3 million of the 10.76 million votes cast in the election of 1918. Mainstream parties now worked hard to capture the female vote – a battle won, it is generally agreed, by the Conservatives. The new political age which the Act of 1918 inaugurated would be dominated by Conservative and Labour, not Conservative and Liberal, parties. The descendants of the successful aristocratic grouping which had started the process in 1832 had finally been relegated to the fringes of British political life.

PART FIVE: CONCLUSION AND ASSESSMENT

THE TWENTIETH CENTURY

Parliamentary Reform is a major topic in the history books only during the nineteenth and early twentieth centuries. Yet, in one sense, its story never ends. It merely throws up constantly changing questions. The Representation of the People Act (1918), despite its huge scope, did not bring down the curtain on the creation of a democratic state. Women from the age of 21 to 30 had to wait until 1928 to receive the vote. Those remaining anomalies, the plural vote and university constituencies, survived the Second World War before being chopped by the post-war Labour government. Not until 1949 did the United Kingdom have a system of one person one vote. Various attempts to reform the House of Lords (see Chronology), most of them frustrated in one way or another, were made in the second half of the twentieth century. No government would come forward with specific proposals for drastically reducing the number of hereditary peers who would sit in the House of Lords until 1998.

Proposals by the Labour party in 1999 for popular nominations to the House of Lords reflected the fussy tinkering over 'fancy franchises' for the Commons in the 1850s and 1860s (see Chapter 5). Both the shape, and the scope, of a reformed second chamber remained obscure at the dawn of the twenty-first century. Constitutional historians, however, exchanged knowing smiles that it was another Cranborne who gained a brief extension of life for a number of hereditary peers during a secret deal with the Labour government and kept his own party leader in the dark. Such party disloyalties were a family trait. It will be recalled that his ancestor had fought Derby and Disraeli tooth and nail over any kind of reform in 1867 (see p. 51).

Meanwhile, arcane discussions of which system of voting is most appropriate for a mature democracy resurfaced in the 1980s and 1990s. For many years it seemed almost as if the sole point of the Liberal party (or Liberal Democrats) was to push proportional representation.

Not surprisingly, as the third party in a 'two-party system' it was the only major grouping which would obviously and directly benefit from it at every election. The climax of the campaign was a portentous report on proportional representation produced by a committee headed by the distinguished historian, politician and – yes – Liberal Democrat life peer, Roy Jenkins, in 1998. Though its elegant phraseology and recondite historical allusions beguiled the literati, it succeeded only in confirming an important lesson from the nineteenth and early twentieth centuries. As debates over the Speaker's Conference recommendations demonstrated long before (see pp. 87–8), it is much easier to agree that the existing system of representation is fallible than to agree how best to improve it. The immediate impact of the Jenkins report on the ordinary voter was nil. The twenty-first century must, no doubt, resolve already anguished debates about the respective powers of a democratically elected national government and that supra-national organisation which pretentiously and inaccurately calls itself 'the European Union', though its unity is dubious and its representation in eastern Europe minimal.

What can we learn from a study of political representation over a period of more than a century? The most important lesson, surely, is that history rarely proceeds in linear fashion. The history of nineteenth-century parliamentary reform is not a story of stately progress from the darkness of corrupt manipulation and highly restricted voting rights to the broad sunlit uplands of open, participatory democracy. Britain had its democrats in the late eighteenth and early nineteenth centuries, but the overwhelming majority of reformers in parliament wanted change in order to frustrate democracy and preserve what they saw as the essentials of good government. These they defined as control by a small, and to a significant degree, unelected and highly educated elite. If government remained in the hands of these paragons, then all would be well. It was of the essence of the Whig creed that great men could be trusted not only to rein in the inevitably autocratic ambitions of the monarchy but also to govern in the interests of all classes.

For much of the eighteenth and nineteenth centuries, the Whig view of the political world proved remarkably resilient. At Westminster, Britain remained governed by great landowners at least until the end of the nineteenth century. Those landowners participated in a programme of substantial reform, political, economic and social, which did much to ensure that Britain (if not the Irish element in the United Kingdom) successfully managed the transition from a rural to an industrial and commercial state without violent revolution.

SAFETY IN NUMBERS

It is important to remember that what was essentially a reformist creed remained undemocratic. Democracy, as one Whig supporter said, is 'fatal to the purposes for which government exists'. Throughout the nineteenth century, therefore, the key reform question was: 'Whom is it safe to enfranchise?' It was the definition of 'safe' which changed rather than the ultimate objective. The enfranchisement clauses of the so-called Great Reform Act were carefully designed to include the fearfully conservative lower-middle classes and to exclude working people, many of whose leaders called stridently for democracy [*Doc. 7*]. In this objective, the Whigs succeeded brilliantly, ensuring that the six points of the People's Charter would not be achieved in the 1830s and 1840s. The second Reform Act came about partly for tactical reasons (see Chapter 6) but it would not have become law had the legislature not recognised the essential 'respectability' of the skilled adult males who were its main beneficiaries. The householder franchise of 1867 horrified far more than Robert Lowe and the Adullamites, but civilisation did not come crashing about their ears in the 1870s. The changes of 1884–85 are likewise best explained as a logical extension to the rural areas of a principle which had been found fit for the purpose in the towns. The main areas of contention were political, with Conservatives outmanoeuvring Liberals over redistribution (see pp. 68–71). The message remained clear enough: a household suffrage was safely inclusive.

Legislation extending educational provision for the lower orders tumbled forth in the last quarter of the nineteenth century, with important Acts passed in 1870, 1876, 1881, 1891 and 1902. Nothing so crass as 'education for citizenship' was put on to the curriculum. However, the objective of acculturing the British working classes within what the elite taught them was an effective representative system was clear enough. History made an increasingly important contribution to scholarship in the late nineteenth and early twentieth centuries. The political, rather than the economic and social, perspective was dominant for most school children. In addition to encouraging children to memorise names and dates of monarchs and leading politicians (which they generally hated), history also recounted some rattling good yarns (which they generally lapped up). Central to the 'story' was Britain's imperial destiny: a group of small islands on the fringes of north-west Europe which gave valuable lessons to the rest of the world. Britain had become the world's first industrial nation and was in the process of becoming the largest empire the world had ever seen. Stories of imperial 'derring-do' seem to have been immensely popular. They were always high on the list of prizes given for attendance and good behaviour at Sunday Schools, for example.

EMPIRE, PROGRESS AND MYTH

The essential message was never less than heavily implicit. Not only did Britain rule the waves; it ruled benevolently, conveying to those fortunate enough to be colonised by it the incalculable benefits of Christianity and representative government. The avoidance of political revolution, moreover, was a trick not managed by any of its main competitors. One Manchester businessman, Absolom Watkin, was gloating as early as 1853: 'never have I seen clearer evidence of general well-being. Our country is, no doubt, in a most happy and prosperous state. Free trade, peace and freedom' [7 *p. 290*].

The empire was not acquired entirely peacefully, of course, but Britain did avoid major European wars (with the brief exception of the Crimean War) in the century which used to frame so many history syllabuses: 1815–1914. To Watkin's trilogy, a late Victorian or Edwardian statesman would have added a fourth – progress. Britain's nineteenth-century history was the story from a lesser to a greater state: more wealth, more international influence, more territory, much more prestige. And as the country progressed, so its government became more representative. Its aristocracy, never a closed caste, had assimilated successful businessmen, industrialists, soldiers and lawyers. The House of Commons, dominated by landowners for so long, could at last boast a middle-class majority by the end of the century. The emergence of a Labour party designed to increase direct representation of working men could even be fitted into this progressive model. Working people, having given ample proof of their respectability and good intentions, would, in their time, produce statesmen at least as interested in winning recognition from the political *status quo* as in changing it.

Much of the beneficent image was, of course, myth. However, myth is often as important as reality, especially when it shapes a nation's perception of itself. The reality was that, with 65 per cent of men and no women able to vote in parliamentary elections, Britain had one of the least representative franchises in the modern world on the eve of the First World War (see Chapters 9 and 10). Successive extensions of the franchise were accompanied by continuity as well as change. They left the power structure more or less intact, controlled, as it still was, by a privileged male elite which had been educated in schools which were light years away from the elementary establishments created and expanded under legislation passed since 1870. Women property owners, eminently respectable and well-educated, did not get the vote before 1914 largely because progressive politicians feared, with good reason, that the consequences of enfranchising female householders would be to the advantage of the Conservative party rather than of them.

Far from progressing in stately, inexorable fashion towards the 'achievement' of democracy, then, Britain was jerked into it by the horrendous discontinuity of the First World War. Respectability, along with so much else, died on the Western Front. Young men considered too poor or too weakly established in life to merit the vote were dying for their country in their hundreds of thousands. Women showed themselves at least as patriotic as men, and did far more than 'their bit' during the war. The context of the debates on franchise reform in 1917 is entirely different from those of the 1830s, 1860s or 1880s. What one historian has called the 'patriotic consensus' now overbore all reservations. Only a smallish minority on the Conservative side remained worried about creating a democratic electorate prone, as one agent put it, to 'support any demagogue however brazen and any scheme however wild which appeals to their [sic] selfish interests' [138 *p. 895*]. Democracy was now assumed by most MPs to be not just acceptable but far superior to those alien doctrines, socialism and Bolshevism, which were stamping their malign impact on central and eastern Europe just as universal manhood suffrage and majority female voting were being established in Britain. Democracy thus arrived in Britain in 1918 in a rush and safely, but tardily and unheroically. The achievement was a characteristically oblique one. Britain remained less progressively benevolent than its leaders liked to pretend.

PART SIX: DOCUMENTS

DOCUMENT 1 TOM PAINE ATTACKS CUSTOM AND
PRECEDENT AS A VALID BASIS FOR
GOVERNMENT AND REPRESENTATION

Tom Paine's Rights of Man, *published in two parts in 1791–92, deserves to be called the 'Bible of British Radicalism'. It played the leading role in educating working people by popularising those democratic ideas about 'government by consent', derived from the European Enlightenment which had long been discussed by rationalists and intellectuals. It also attacked the institutions of monarchy and aristocracy. The second part introduced some genuinely novel features, such as ideas of a graduated income tax to help fund a range of welfare schemes. It is not surprising that the book was rapidly condemned as a seditious libel. In this extract, Paine attempts to refute the arguments of his great antagonist Edmund Burke, whose* Reflections on the Revolution in France *(1790) had alerted property owners in Britain to the dangers of democracy implicit in the recent upheaval in France. Paine argues that people cannot be bound by custom or precedent. His attacks on the aristocracy also convey that pungent combination of brilliant polemical writing and raw abuse which so alarmed the authorities. Note also the casual anti-Semitic libel which excited far less attention in the 1790s than it would do in the 1990s.*

There never did, there never will, and there never can, exist a Parliament, or any description of men, or any generation of men, in any country, possessed of the right or the power of binding and controuling [*sic*] posterity to '*the end of time*'. ... Every age and generation must be as free to act for itself *in all cases* as the ages and generations which preceded it. The vanity and presumption of governing beyond the grave is the most ridiculous and insolent of all tyrannies. ... Every generation is, and must be, competent to all the purposes which its occasions require. It is the living, and not the dead, that are to be accommodated. ... I am contending for the rights of the *living*, and against their being willed away, and controuled and contracted for, by the manuscript assumed authority of the dead; and Mr. Burke is contending for the authority of the dead over the rights and freedom of the living. ... It requires but a very small glance of thought to perceive that altho' laws made in one generation often continue in force through succeeding generations, yet that they continue to derive their force from the consent of the living....

That, then, which is called Aristocracy in some countries and Nobility in others arose out of the Governments founded upon conquest. ... Aristocracy is kept up by family tyranny and injustice ... the idea of hereditary legislators is as inconsistent as that of hereditary judges, or hereditary juries; and as absurd as an hereditary mathematician, or an hereditary wise man ... a body of men, holding themselves accountable to nobody, ought not to be trusted by anybody ... [Aristocracy] is continuing the uncivilised principle of Government founded in conquest, and the base idea of having property in man, and governing him by personal right. ... Aristocracy has a tendency to degenerate the human species. By the universal oeconomy of nature it is known, and by the instance of the Jews it is proved, that the human species has a tendency to degenerate, in any small number of persons, when separated from the general stock of society, and inter-marrying constantly with each other.

Tom Paine, *The Rights of Man*, Everyman edn, 1915, pp. 12–13 and 61–3.

DOCUMENT 2   ASSERTING THE RIGHTS OF
             'CONSTITUTIONAL ENGLISHMEN'

This comes from a speech made at a radical meeting by a printer from the Yorkshire town of Dewsbury during the strong anti-government protests in the summer of 1819, which reached a climax in the so-called 'Peterloo Massacre'. It indicates the importance to many skilled workers of tradition and precedent. They felt that it was the government which was subverting the old order and using corrupt powers to enslave Englishmen. This radical tradition asserted a patriotic stance and was, in many respects, different from that which drew its inspiration from the European Enlightenment and the French Revolution.

Let us tell them what Constitution we admire – what constitution we are anxious to live under – and what Constitution we will cheerfully obey. It is the English Constitution. ... This Constitution, on which English law ought to be founded, is the Constitution which we claim, demand and insist upon; and not the laws which have subverted this Constitution by taxing men without their consent, by withholding justice, by demanding excessive bail, and punishing numerous individuals without a trial by their peers.

Leeds Mercury, 7 August 1819, quoted in [29], p. 75.

DOCUMENT 3   A RADICAL ATTACK ON THE
UNREFORMED POLITICAL SYSTEM

John Wade, who was originally a journeyman in the wool trade, would today be described as an investigative journalist. He edited the radical journal Gorgon during the Peterloo years and was also a formidable researcher. He used his skills to compile a massive dossier of pensions, sinecures and wealth rapidly acquired in the public service. To his research skills, he added literary ones which drew on the polemical inheritance of Tom Paine to produce a formidable attack on 'Old Corruption'. This extract from a chapter entitled 'State of the Representation' is from his most famous work and comes at the end of a book which has already dealt with alleged graft and corruption in the public service, the police establishment of London, the extravagance of monarchy and court, 'robbery of charitable foundations', the Bank of England, 'the established clergy' (whom he found a particularly juicy target), aristocracy and the East India Company.

We come now to the root of all evil – the corrupt state of the representation. The fatal prediction that the liberties of the people could only be destroyed by a corrupt House of Commons has been fully verified, and we now behold, in the calamitous state of the country – in the ruin of industry – in the extreme indigence of one class and the bloated opulence of another – in weak men, recommended only by their servility and wickedness, directing the affairs of a great nation – all the evils resulting from a government, founded neither on the virtue, talents, opinion, nor property of the community. ... [T]he House of Commons ... is not only unconstitutional, it is glaringly absurd and ridiculous: it is founded on no rational principle of either population, intelligence, or property. There is Old Sarum, for instance. Of this borough, nothing remains but a *thorn bush*, yet it has a nominal bailiff and burgesses, and returns two members of parliament.

John Wade, *The Black Book; or, Corruption Unmasked*, London, 1820, pp. 413–14.

DOCUMENT 4   A TURNING OF THE REFORMERS' TIDE?

This brief comment from an annual publication not notably favourable to the reformers' cause was made in the wake of Lord John Russell's attempt to guide parliamentary reform through the Commons in 1822. Russell and the Whigs were out of office at this time and had no realistic expectation of success. However, this attempt did put reform back onto the 'respectable' political agenda of Westminster.

The strength which the minority mustered on this occasion, gave them more rational hopes of ultimate, though remote, triumph than had been entertained for thirty years. A circumstance which added not a little to the exultation of the friends of reform, was, that they now saw in their ranks several young men, the heirs of great families, whose support would, by and by, prove an immense acquisition of force.

Annual Register, 64 (1822), pp. 78–9.

DOCUMENT 5   A REFORM PETITION TO PARLIAMENT

Petitioning was the legitimate and acknowledged route by which grievances and proposals might be brought to parliament either by, or on behalf of, those who were not directly represented there. The volume, and tenor, of petitions was regarded as a reliable weather-gauge of public opinion. Petitions such as the one below from 'the nobility, gentry, and others of the county of Norfolk' on 3 January 1823 would be expected to carry weight with a landowners' parliament. The context was widespread agricultural distress and the Norfolk petitioners were aligning themselves with the mainstream of radical opinion in attacking 'Corruption'. The reaction was significant. Michael Taylor, MP for Durham City, was a Whig lawyer who supported parliamentary reform. His intervention was intended to demonstrate that the Whigs could be trusted to handle the reform question in a measured and moderate manner and not to set off reactions such as those in France in the 1790s which had proved so damaging to the Whig reformers' cause.

... your petitioners ... are now impelled by their well-known, indescribable and unmerited sufferings, to approach your honourable house with an humble prayer, that you will be pleased to adopt the best means of relieving them from those sufferings ... in proceeding to suggest those means, which they do with the greatest respect and deference, your humble petitioners cannot disguise from themselves ... that they entertain a fixed opinion, that this now unhappy country owes all its calamities to the predominance of certain particular families, who, since the passing of the Septennial act, have, by degrees, appropriated to themselves a large part of the property and revenue of the whole nation; and who have, at last, by taxes, debts and changes in the currency, involved themselves as well as the whole of this industrious community, in difficulties too great to be removed by the hand of time, or any but the most vigorous measures of legislation. ... Your petitioners, therefore, most humbly pray, that your honourable House will be pleased to pass an act for causing an efficient reform in the Commons House of parliament. [The petition went on to call for the use of church property to help liquidate government debt.] A reduction of the standing army. ... A total abolition of all sinecures, pensions, grants, and emoluments, not merited by public service. ... A sale of numerous public estates, commonly called crown lands ...

Mr M. A. Taylor said ... Though he had been for many years, and still was, a steady advocate for parliamentary reform, he was sure that there was scarcely one gentleman in that House who would not consider such a petition adverse, instead of being favourable to that great cause. ... A petition containing such a mass of absurdities, such a tissue of false statements, and such a farrago of inconclusive reasoning could only be offered to the House by the firm and decided enemies of parliamentary reform. It went to a direct revolution in church and state.

Hansard, 2nd series, vol. 8 (1823), cols 1254–6.

DOCUMENT 6   THE DUKE OF WELLINGTON AND
PARLIAMENTARY REFORM IN 1830

This extract is from the journal of one of London's most celebrated political hostesses, Harriet Arbuthnot (1794–1834). She was the wife of Charles Arbuthnot, who had been ambassador at Constantinople and later became Patronage Secretary in Liverpool's Tory government. This role gave his wife access to a great deal of 'insider knowledge' and her journals are full of indiscreet gossip. Not only was Mrs Arbuthnot a close friend of the Duke of Wellington (some alleged she was also his mistress), she was also an uncompromising Tory who hated the prospect of reform. Here she reflects on political prospects in the light of recent disturbances after the Lords rejected the Whig reform bill. Her hopes that Wellington's ministry would survive were, of course, dashed. He resigned office later in the month.

7 November 1830: We hear the radicals are determined to make a riot, the Lord Mayor has written to the Duke to say he cannot answer for his safety unless he comes with an escort, he gets quantities of letters every day telling him he will be murdered, the King is very much frightened, the Queen cries half the day with fright at the idea of going; altogether, we are in a nice predicament. And all *about nothing*, for it is quite preposterous to imagine that the idle vagabonds who compose the mob of London care a pin about Parliamentary Reform. What they want is plunder. ...

The Duke is greatly affected by all this state of affairs. He feels that beginning reform is beginning revolution, that therefore he must stem the tide as long as possible, and that all he has to do is to see *when* & *how* it will be best for the country that he shd. resign. He thinks he cannot till he is beat in the H of Commons. He talked about this with me yesterday and I told him that, in my opinion, if he really & honestly believed that the reformers obtaining power wd lead to revolution, he was bound in honour as an honest man to resist that to the last & to keep his place as long as he cd possibly be supported. He seemed to agree in that and I hope he will do it. We hear the Opposition are calculating confidently upon coming in, but that the most sober among them are somewhat alarmed at the difficulties they will have to contend with, at the violence of party in England and the disturbed & wretched state of France & the Netherlands, all of which will be aggravated by the overturn of the Duke.

Francis Bamford and the 7th Duke of Wellington (eds), *The Journal of Mrs Arbuthnot, 1820–1832*, Macmillan, London, 1950, vol. 2, pp. 398–9.

DOCUMENT 7   AN EARLY RADICAL ATTACK ON THE 'GREAT' REFORM ACT

Henry Hetherington (1762–1849) was one of the most impressive radical journalists of the age and a leading figure in what has been called the 'war of the unstamped press'. The 1832 Act divided radical opinion. Some considered it inadequate but a necessary first step to real reform. Hetherington took an entirely different view. Not only did the 1832 Reform Act do nothing for working people; it was, in effect, intended to prop up the old world of property and privilege rather than usher in a new one of representation and political rights. Hetherington was one of the key figures linking the democratic ideas of the more radical reformers in the early 1830s with Chartism. He was later a leading supporter of rationalist, 'education', Chartism. Note the savage irony with which he invests the word 'great'.

... with a little instinctive sense of self-preservation, have the Whigs manufactured a 'great measure'. They know that the old system could not last, and desiring to establish another as like it as possible, and also to keep their places, they framed the BILL, in the hope of drawing to the feudal aristocracy and yeomanry of the counties a large reinforcement of the middle class. The Bill was, in effect, an invitation to the shopocrats of the enfranchised towns to join the Whiggocrats of the country, and make common cause with them in keeping down the people, and thereby to quell the rising spirit of democracy in England.

Henry Hetherington, *Poor Man's Guardian*, 27 October 1832.

DOCUMENT 8   PARLIAMENTARY REFORM ASSERTED TO BE NO LONGER A CLASS QUESTION

By the late 1850s, social tension had perceptibly slackened and conflicts were less frequently characterised as between class and class. In such an atmosphere, the enfranchisement of sober, educated members of the working class seemed much less threatening. Increasing the franchise became the means of creating an 'inclusive' political nation for the benefit of all. The following contribution, by the son of 'Earl Grey of the Reform Act', is typical of the arguments advanced by wealthy reformers in the late 1850s and early 1860s. Notice how important the objective of 'reforming to preserve' remains.

... a new Reform bill ought not, like the former one, to aim at the transfer of a large amount of political power from one class of society to another, since this is no longer necessary. ... A reform is wanted ... to interest a larger proportion of people in the Constitution, by investing them with political rights, without disturbing the existing balance of power; to discourage bribery at elections, without giving more influence to the arts of demagogues; to strengthen the legitimate authority of Executive Government, and at the same time to guard against its being abused; to render the distribution of the Parliamentary franchise less unequal and less anomalous, but yet carefully to preserve that character which has hitherto belonged to the House of Commons, from including among its Members men representing all the different classes of society, and all the different interests and opinions to be found in the Nation.

Third Earl Grey, *Parliamentary Government, 1858*, quoted in H. J. Hanham (ed.), *The Nineteenth-century Constitution*, Cambridge University Press, Cambridge, 1969, p. 271.

DOCUMENT 9   JOHN STUART MILL'S VIEWS ON 'ONE MAN, ONE VOTE'

John Stuart Mill (1806–73) was one of the leading progressive political thinkers of the mid-Victorian period. A few years later, he would be one of the first from the political elite to argue the case of votes for women. It is worth remembering these facts when reading the document which follows. To readers almost a century and a half later, the argument that citizens should have political influence in proportion to their political knowledge and understanding may seem hopelessly backward-looking. Mill was, of course, writing in an age before mass state education but his argument that voters should be able to demonstrate basic understanding of the issues on which their views are being sought needs more careful, and developed, rebuttal than it generally gets in an age of mass democracy and cultural relativism. This piece was written as a contribution to the debate on the Earl of Derby's unsuccessful parliamentary reform bill of 1859.

The possession and the exercise of political, and among others of electoral, rights, is one of the chief instruments both of moral and of intellectual training for the popular mind; and all governments must be regarded as extremely imperfect, until every one who is required to obey the laws, has a voice, or the prospect of a voice, in their enactment and administration.

But ought everyone to have an *equal* voice? This is a totally different proposition; and in my judgment as palpably false, as the other is true and important.

Here it is that I part company, on the question of principle, with the democratic reformers. Agreeing with them in looking forward to universal suffrage as an ultimate aim, I altogether dissent from their advocacy of electoral districts, understood as a means of giving equal weight to the vote of every individual. ...

If it is asserted that all persons ought to be equal in every description of right recognised by society, I answer, not until all are equal in worth as human beings. It is the fact, that one person is *not* as good as another; and it is reversing all the rule of rational conduct, to attempt to raise a political fabric on a supposition which is at variance with fact. Putting aside for the moment the consideration of moral worth, of which, though more important even than intellectual, it is not so easy to find an available test; a person who cannot read is not as good, for the purpose of human life, as one who can. ... A person who can read, write and calculate, but who knows nothing of the properties of natural objects, or of other places and countries, or of the human beings who have lived before him, or of the ideas, opinions, and practices of his fellow-creatures generally, is not so good as the person who knows these things. ...

There is no justification for making the less educated the slave, or serf, or mere dependent of the other. The subjection of any one individual or class to another, is always and necessarily disastrous in its effects on both. That power should be exercised over any portion of mankind without any obligation of consulting them, is only tolerable while they are in an infantine, or a semi-barbarous state. In any civilised condition, power ought never to be exempt from the necessity of appealing to the reason, and recommending itself ... to the conscience and feelings, of the governed. In the present state of society, and under representative institutions, there is no mode of imposing this necessity on the ruling classes, as towards all other persons in the community, except by giving every one a vote. But there is a wide interval between refusing votes to the great majority, and acknowledging in each individual among them a right to have his vote counted for exactly as much as the vote of the most highly educated person in the community.

John Stuart Mill, 'Thoughts on Parliamentary Reform', February 1859, published in *Essays and Politics and Culture* (1963 edition), Doubleday & Co., Garden City, NY, pp. 315–16.

DOCUMENT 10   GLADSTONE CONFIRMS HIS CONVERSION
                TO PARLIAMENTARY REFORM

This much-quoted speech to the House of Commons is important for far more than its pomposity and circumlocution. Gladstone was Chancellor of the Exchequer and was recognised on all sides as the most likely successor to the leadership once Palmerston and Russell had retired or died. If Gladstone were prepared to sponsor reform, therefore, its chances appeared much brighter. Gladstone was no democrat, and never became one. He asserted his preference for aristocratic rule as government by 'the best' but he became convinced of the value of a wider franchise partly on moral grounds – many working men were now worthy of the vote – and partly on the practical consideration that government which had the explicit approval of a large proportion of the population could claim greater authority. Notice Gladstone's emphasis on enfranchising only a 'limited portion' of the working classes.

Every man who is not presumably incapacitated by some consideration of personal unfitness or of political danger is morally entitled to come within the pale of the Constitution. Of course, in giving utterance to such a proposition, I do not recede from the protest I have previously made against sudden, or violent, or excessive ... change. ... What are the qualities which fit a man for the exercise of a privilege such as the franchise? Self-command, self-control, respect for order, patience under suffering, confidence in the law, regard for superiors. ... I am now speaking only of a limited portion of the working class. ... It has been given to us of this generation to witness ... the most blessed of all social processes; I mean the process which unites together not the interests only but the feelings of all the several classes of the community, and throws back into the shadows of oblivion those discords by which they were kept apart from one other. ... I know of nothing which can contribute to that union, to the welfare of the commonwealth ... than that hearts should be bound together by a reasonable extension ... among selected portions of the people, of every benefit, and every privilege that can justly be conferred on them.

William Gladstone, House of Commons, 11 May 1864, *Hansard*, 3rd series, vol. 175, cols. 324–7.

DOCUMENT 11 A WORKING MAN DEFENDS THE NEED TO EXTEND THE FRANCHISE TO WORKING MEN IN 1867

This speech was made by a skilled worker – a brassfinisher – from the northeast. It neatly encapsulates two critical elements in the working-class case for reform. First, skilled workers were perfectly sure that they were responsible enough, and certainly informed enough, to be able to exercise their vote wisely. Secondly, into the 1860s and beyond, they preserved those themes of radical patriotism and liberty through reform which had been such a critical part of the radical case from the end of the eighteenth century.

Their opponents were afraid that if the working classes were admitted to the franchise, they would Frenchify or Americanise the institutions of the country.

But he could assure those opponents that the working men were too much endeared to liberty and institutions for which their forefathers fought and laboured, to change them for those of France; and however much they may sympathise with their American brethren, they still loved the glorious constitution of their own country (Cheers). No, the working classes valued too highly the liberties for which their forefathers fought and bled to change them for those of any foreign land.

Robert Warden, speech at a reform meeting in Newcastle-on-Tyne, February 1867, reported in *Newcastle Weekly Chronicle*, 2 February 1867, quoted in [59], p. 266.

DOCUMENT 12   THE FIRST PARLIAMENTARY
INTERCHANGE ON WOMEN'S SUFFRAGE

The rapid changes which transformed Disraeli's 1867 Reform Bill emboldened John Stuart Mill to ask why women should not be included. His proposal was modest in that he pressed the case of 'spinsters and widows' alone in this debate, although his writings made clear that he favoured giving the vote to women irrespective of marital status. Notice the extent to which both the contribution in favour of votes for women and the contribution against accepted the notion of 'separate spheres' for women. What women might say, or think, was almost invariably refracted through the prism of their natural, and separate, roles. For brief detail on J. S. Mill, see the introduction to Document 9 above. His opponent, E. K. Karslake, had a very brief parliamentary career. He became Conservative MP for Colchester at a by-election in February 1867 and was defeated at the general election of 1868 when Liberals took both the borough seats. Mill's amendment was rejected by 196 votes to 73, though the list of the substantial minority voting with him included some distinguished names, including Edward Baines, John Bright and Henry Labouchere and at least one surprising one, Lt. Gen. Jonathan Peel, who had resigned from Derby's Cabinet over the decision to press ahead with reform (see p. 51).

JOHN STUART MILL: There is nothing to distract our attention from the simple question, whether there is any adequate justification for continuing to exclude an entire half of the community, not only from admission, but from the capability of ever being admitted within the pale of the Constitution, though they may fulfil all the conditions legally and constitutionally sufficient in every case but theirs. Sir, within the limits of our Constitution, this is a solitary case. There is no other example of an exclusion which is absolute. ... The difficulty which most people feel on this subject is not a practical objection; there is nothing practical about it; it is a mere feeling – a feeling of strangeness; this proposal is so new; at least they think so, though this is a mistake; it is a very old proposal. Well, Sir, strangeness is a thing which wears off; some things were strange enough to many of us three months ago which are not at all so now. ... And as for novelty, we live in a world of novelties; the despotism of custom is on the wane; we are not now satisfied with knowing what a thing is, we ask what it ought to be; and in this House at least, I am bound to believe that an appeal lies from custom to a higher tribunal, in which reason is judge. ... Sir, the time is now come when, unless women are raised to the level of men, men will be pulled down to theirs. The women of a man's family are either a stimulus and a support to his highest aspirations, or a drag upon them. You may keep them ignorant of politics, but you cannot prevent them from concerning themselves with the least respectable part of politics – its personalities; if they do not understand and cannot enter into the man's feelings of public duty, they do care about his personal interest. ... They will be an influence always at hand, co-operating with the man's selfish promptings, lying in wait for his moral irresolution, and doubling the strength of every temptation. ... Sir, it is true that women have great power. It is part of my case that they have great power; but that they have it under the worst possible conditions because it is indirect, and therefore irresponsible. I want to make this great power a responsible power. ...

Amendment proposed, in page 2, line 16, to leave out the word 'man' in order to insert the word 'person'.

MR E. K. KARSLAKE: He certainly expected from the hon. Member for Westminster [Mill] reasoning of a much more logical kind than any he had yet used in respect to this question. He thought that the Committee would come to the opinion that the hon. Gentleman was wrong in his first principles. In one of his very able works the hon. Member had laid it down that there was no greater difference between a woman and a man than there was between two human beings, one with red hair and one with black. ... He humbly begged to differ from him, for while he believed that a man qualified to possess the franchise would be ennobled by its possession, woman, in his humble opinion, would be almost debased or degraded by it. She would be in danger of losing those admirable attributes of her sex – namely her gentleness, her affection, and her domesticity. ... As not a lady in Essex had asked him to support the proposition in favour of a female franchise, and believing that women in other parts of England were equally indifferent on the subject, he came to the conclusion that the women of this country would prefer to remain as they were, being content with the happy homes and advantages they now possessed.

John Stuart Mill and E. K. Karslake, House of Commons, 20 May 1867, *Hansard*, 3rd series, vol. 187, cols 817–33.

DOCUMENT 13   JOHN BRIGHT ARGUES FOR A SECRET BALLOT

Bright had been a supporter of the ballot since early in his career. It was not an issue which aroused all radicals and some of the keenest supporters of an extension in the franchise were hostile to it. The ballot had been one of the Chartists' six points, of course, but support for it had waned before Bright convinced Gladstone that the Liberal government should support a measure which would reduce bribery and the risk of corruption.

I regard the question of the ballot as of first importance. Whether I look to the excessive cost of elections, or to the tumult which so often attends them, or to the unjust and cruel pressure which is so frequently brought to bear upon the less independent class of voters, I am persuaded that the true interest of the public and of freedom will be served by the adoption of the system of secret and free voting.

Election address to the Electors of Birmingham, August 1868. George Barnett Smith (ed.), *The Life and Speeches of John Bright MP*, 2 vols, London, 1881, vol. 2, p. 343.

DOCUMENT 14   IN DEFENCE OF INFLUENCE

The following document is included to show that some MPs, at least, were prepared to state that the honest relationship between a landlord and his tenants implied unswerving political loyalty. The splendidly named John Samuel Wanley Sawbridge-Erle-Drax was MP for the borough of Wareham in Dorset almost continuously from 1832 to 1880 (he lost the election of 1857 by 143 votes to 140 before being returned unopposed in 1859). Drax was an independently minded Whig-Liberal in the 1830s and 1840s before transferring his allegiance to the Conservatives early in the 1850s. His change of political heart seems to have mattered little more to the voters of Wareham than the fact that he considered attendance at Westminster a rather irksome business and attended on average about once in a parliamentary session. His constituency had 300–400 voters between 1832 and 1867 and over 900 after the Second Reform Act. Here he makes quite clear his views about the obligations of a voting tenantry.

Electors of Wareham! I understand that some evil-disposed person has been circulating a report that I wish my tenants, and other persons dependent on me, to vote according to their conscience. This is a dastardly lie; calculated to injure me. I have no wish of the sort. I wish, and I intend, that these persons shall vote for me.

Quoted in [78], p. 52.

DOCUMENT 15   THE CONCEPT OF MANHOOD SUFFRAGE

The 1867 Reform Act did not quieten demands from working men for further reform. It should not be thought, however, that the inevitable next step was universal manhood suffrage. Another important strand of continuity in radical activity was the notion that voters should contribute to the well-being of society. Voting, on this characterisation, was a socially active process. Here a Newcastle carpenter draws the relevant distinction in a speech made in early 1873.

The men who swept the streets or shaped the wood, or hammered the iron, or hewed the coal, were men honourably doing their duty, and men who ought to possess the rights of citizenship. If any one ought to be excluded from the exercise of these, it ought to be those men who did nothing for the benefit of society.

Reported in *Newcastle Chronicle*, 5 May 1873, and quoted in [59], p. 286.

DOCUMENT 16   CONSERVATIVE ORGANISATION IN
               RESPONSE TO THE 1867 REFORM ACT

This extract comes from a biography of Disraeli. It was written by the son of John Eldon Gorst, the Conservative party's election agent in the 1870s. It gives a valuable insight into the practical steps which needed to be taken to make an impression on all constituencies, including those which had rarely returned Conservative MPs. Conservative revival was grounded in the necessity to broaden the base of party loyalty beyond the English counties and their, still overwhelmingly propertied, voters.

The first step to be taken was the organisation of local committees in the towns and country divisions. In order to carry out this object it was necessary to pay a personal visit to every constituency throughout the country. Arrangements were made to meet the most influential local Conservatives at each place, and to persuade them to form a committee for the purpose of propagating Conservative principles and arranging about a local candidate. These committees, when once they had been established, rapidly grew into Conservative associations. Intelligent working-men were easily persuaded to join them, and they are now known everywhere by the common appellation 'Conservative Working-Men's Associations'. In the counties these associations always remained aristocratic in character, and chiefly consisted of country gentlemen and the superior class of farmers; but in the manufacturing districts of counties like Yorkshire and Lancashire, and in large towns such as Birmingham and Sheffield, they spread at the most astonishing speed among the masses of the electorate.

Harold E. Gorst, *Earl of Beaconsfield*, pp. 126–7, quoted in [78], pp. 114–15.

DOCUMENT 17   THE SECRET BALLOT COMES INTO
OPERATION

Gladstone's government introduced the secret ballot in 1872 in the teeth of strong pressure from the House of Lords. The upper house backed down only in the face of a threat by the Liberals to call a general election. The Liberals also had to accept that the Act would only operate, in the first instance, until 1880. The new form of voting was tried out for the first time at a by-election held for the Yorkshire (West Riding) borough of Pontefract. The newspaper account below indicates what a change in the culture of elections it brought in. Ideas of 'virtual democracy', whereby non-voters could nevertheless participate in elections by expressing their views (sometimes in a rowdy, drunken manner) around the hustings, were swept away. Elections – outwardly at least – became a sober, serious, respectable business.

No bands of music paraded the town. No colours or banners were seen in procession. The church bells were silent. ... Both at Pontefract and Knottingley the topic was the dullness of the election. 'It hardly seemed like an election', the tradespeople said; and they were right.

The Times, 16 August 1872, quoted in [84], p. 86.

DOCUMENT 18   ACTIVE CITIZENSHIP THE TOUCHSTONE
FOR THE VOTE

It is often forgotten how few working men supported democracy in the 1870s. Voters without proper education or who were in a state of dependence on others, they argued, would weaken the campaign for political liberties because they could easily be coerced. The notion of the independent, 'freeborn' Englishman, whose rights had been asserted at least since the 1640s, continued to hold sway. None in a state of 'dependency', therefore, could be safely entrusted with the vote. The views of this miner were typical. Notice the concern that those who were dependent on others might be 'used' by them.

Although they objected to paupers [as voters], they sympathised with them on account of their poverty, and readily admitted that they might have as good principles at heart as any on that ground: but still, being under the control and influence of the poor law authorities, it was felt that they could never exercise their will like free man, and might be used to check the good which free men in other ranks of life might be striving for.

From a speech by C. Kidd, at a meeting of local miners held on Durham Racecourse, 14 June 1873, quoted in [59], pp. 287–8.

DOCUMENT 19   A COMMENTARY ON THE REASONS FOR
THE CONSERVATIVE VICTORY IN THE
ELECTION OF 1874

*The author of this document was a leading Liberal thinker. His analysis thus
needs to be read with some caution. It is nevertheless very acute. It deals with
the lessening attractions of Liberalism for both the middle classes and the new
voters. The author's assumption that the well-educated and reflective working
man would naturally vote for Liberal, 'progressive' policies whereas workers
with less political sophistication were easy meat for Conservative 'demagogism'
was widespread in Liberal circles. It is worth stressing also how many middle-
class voters with industrial and professional jobs in the towns cast their votes
not in the boroughs but in counties like Middlesex, Surrey, Warwickshire or
Lancashire. These were the types of county seat in which, before 1874, the
Liberals tended to do relatively well.*

The real truth is that the middle-class, or its effective strength, has swung
round to Conservatism. ... When we look at the poll in the City of London, in
Westminster, in Middlesex, in Surrey, in Liverpool, Manchester, Leeds and
Sheffield, in the metropolitan boroughs and in the home counties, in all the
centres of middle-class industry, wealth and cultivation, we see one unmis-
takeable fact, that the rich trading class, and the comfortable middle-class has
grown distinctly Conservative. ... The sleek citizens, who pour forth daily
from thousands and thousands of smug villas round London, Manchester and
Liverpool ... believe the country will do very well as it is. ... [The Liberal sup-
porter] has been wont to smile at the vision of the Conservative working man.
Perhaps he smiles no longer. He has had a good deal to do with the making of
the Conservative working man. ... [In the textile districts] where political
intelligence is not very broad, where trade questions are very absorbing, and
where the factory system stimulates a local and domestic partisanship the
Conservative working man may be found in droves.

Frederick Harrison, 'Conservative reaction', *Fortnightly Review*, March
1874, pp. 303–5.

DOCUMENT 20   THE FORMATION OF THE NATIONAL
LIBERAL FEDERATION

*The National Liberal Federation was formed in 1877 on principles which had
been developed in Birmingham which, under the direction of Joseph
Chamberlain, had proved extremely successful in resisting the challenge of the
Conservatives. After the 1874 election defeat, the need to rebuild Liberal
fortunes was urgent. The basis of this rebuilding was respect for the ideas and
views of local associations and members, including respectable workers and*

nonconformists who had been at the heart of so many urban organisations from the 1840s onwards.

The objects of the Association are the return of Liberal members to Parliament and to local governing bodies, and the general promotion of Liberal principles. Its *organisation* is entirely representative in character. The central body, having charge of the whole direction of its affairs, is termed the 'Committee of Six Hundred', and is composed of members freely chosen at public meetings of Liberals, held annually in each municipal ward of the borough. ...

The principles upon which the Association is based are, therefore the following:

(a) The whole body of Liberals in the borough is recognised as the constituency of the Association, and every Liberal has the vote in the election of its committees.

(b) Political responsibility, and the ultimate power of control, belong to the largest representative body, and the policy of the Association is loyally guided by its decision.

(c) The decision of the majoriy, in the selection of candidates and other matters of practical business, is regarded as binding upon those who consent to be nominated, as well as upon the general body of members.

(d) A broad and generous meaning is given to Liberalism, and no subject of public or political importance is excluded from its deliberations.

Proceedings Attending the Formation of the National Federation of Liberal Associations, Birmingham, 1877, and quoted in [78], pp. 134–5.

DOCUMENT 21   CORRUPTION IN A PARLIAMENTARY BOROUGH, 1880

The issue of corruption increasingly worried MPs. The revelations of widespread malpractice during the general election of 1880 led directly to the passage of the Corrupt and Illegal Practices Prevention Act in 1883. Here a Royal Commission reports on the extraordinary activities in the borough of Sandwich (comprising the small Kent towns of Sandwich, Deal and Walmer), which had just over 2,000 voters. They took place during a by-election held immediately after the 1880 general election because the successful Liberal candidate had taken a peerage. An experienced election agent from London, Edwin Hughes, was engaged to organise voters for the Conservative candidate C. H. Crompton-Roberts who was attempting to break a long-established Liberal monopoly in the borough. His first action, aimed at getting the favourably disposed drink trade on his side, was to engage 350 public houses as 'committee rooms'. The Conservative candidate won the by-election but the Commissioners' report was damning.

Observing the nature and the manner of the bribery committed ... the general expectation that money would be distributed in bribery, the almost universal willingness ... to accept bribes, the great proportion of the population implicated, the ease with which the most extensive bribery was carried out, the organisation for the purposes of bribery, which was far too facile and complete to be inexperienced, the readiness on the part of many to accept bribes from both sides, and the total absence of a voice to warn, condemn, or denounce, we cannot doubt that electoral corruption had long and extensively prevailed in the borough of Sandwich.

Report of the Royal Commission on electoral malpractice in Sandwich, *Parliamentary Papers*, 1881, vol. 45, p. 15, quoted in [84], p. 154.

DOCUMENT 22   **LIBERAL FEARS OVER THE REDISTRIBUTION OF SEATS IN 1884–85**

George Joachim Goschen (1832–1907) came from a wealthy banking family and was Liberal MP for Ripon (Yorkshire). He had served in Gladstone's 1868–74 government, first as President of the Poor Law Board and then as First Lord of the Admiralty. Increasingly, however, he detached himself from the party leadership, refusing office in Gladstone's second administration, partly because of opposition to extending the county franchise. He believed that the Redistribution of Seats Act passed by Salisbury's Conservative government would damage the Liberal party. The main concern was the removal of most dual constituencies, which destroyed the effective working relations which had developed in many Liberal seats between a Whig and a radical MP. Redistribution did indeed remove 58 seats which had been Liberal after the 1880 general election as against only 37 Conservative, though this was at least partly compensated by the Liberals' much greater representation in the larger boroughs which retained two MPs. Here he reflects the concern of many Liberals that the loss of so many dual-member constituencies would lead to representation on the basis of social class and effective disfranchisement of large minorities. Goschen left Gladstone's Liberal party over Home Rule and sat as a Liberal–Unionist.

I say that in such a transfer of Members the Conservatives, from their own point of view, will be committing a gross error by neglecting the great forces of the middle classes of this country. ... It appears to me that it is not sound Conservative policy to remove power from a certain number of boroughs which stand between the small boroughs and the very large boroughs, in order to concentrate power even on the Tory democracy of the large towns. ... It has been the strength of this constitution and the glory of English politics that in electoral contests the master and his servant, the manufacturer and his foreman and his factory hands, have served on the same Committees, have voted for the same candidates, have canvassed for the same men, and have influenced each other's opinions, not only at the time of the election, but they have had their political education by the combination of all classes together. And are we to change that in the great towns? Are we to have representatives of the Proletariat in the East End of London and of the rich districts in the West? ... I admit that all classes must be represented; but I should wish them to be represented by still remaining together and fighting out their differences between themselves. ... Let us beware that the single-member constituencies do not develop into one class constituencies, whose members will come here feeling themselves responsible, not to the whole people of the country, but to the particular class living in the district by which they are returned.

G. J. Goschen, House of Commons, 4 December 1884, *Hansard*, 3rd series, vol. 294, cols 716–21.

DOCUMENT 23   *THE ECONOMIST* APPLAUDS SINGLE-
MEMBER CONSTITUENCIES

The Economist *took a very different view of single-member constituencies from G. J. Goschen. Founded in 1843 to campaign for the repeal of the Corn Laws, it became one of the most influential journals in favour of free trade and minimal government expenditure. This brought it ever closer to the Conservatives from the 1880s onwards. Its approval for single-member constituencies needs to be read against the likely benefits for Conservatives. Note the importance which the journal attaches to the reduction in the number of uncontested elections. Opportunities for Whig landowners to climb into two-member constituencies as the 'second MP on the ticket' were greatly reduced.*

... the Bill, besides being immensely wide, so wide as to amount, with its corollary, the Franchise Bill, to a pacific revolution, disturbs all personal interests in a way no previous Bill has ever done. With the exception of the sixty or so seats in the boroughs with between 50,000 and 165,000, no seat in the country is unaffected. What with the disfranchisements, and the new franchise, and the increase in Members for large places and the adoption throughout nine-tenths of the Kingdom of the one-member principle, every sitting member will find himself, for one reason or another, addressing a new constituency ... it must not be forgotten that, among other old things, most political organisations perish under the Bill. There will no longer be a Liverpool, but nine Liverpools, often singularly apart in feeling; no longer a Birmingham but seven Birminghams, in one of which Lord Randolph Churchill [the prominent Conservative spokesman] hopes to find a seat. The county members will not only have to attract a new constituency, but to attract a new district, and to secure it without concessions which the existence of the second member often enabled him to make. He will rarely or never be unopposed, for the new Bribery

Act makes elections relatively cheap. ... So great, indeed, will be the disturbance, that we incline to believe the one-member principle the essence of the
new Bill, and to discuss that rather than the slightly over-discussed gain to
Democracy, or to the power of Executive.

The Economist, 4 December 1884. Quoted in J. B. Conacher (ed.), *The Emergence of Parliamentary Democracy in the Nineteenth Century*, John Wiley,
New York, 1971, pp. 163–4.

DOCUMENT 24   SUFFRAGETTE DISILLUSION WITH THE
LABOUR PARTY

*This statement from Christabel Pankhurst (1880–1958), the daughter of
Emmeline and a trained lawyer who was prevented from practising on gender
grounds, indicates why supporters of votes for women became disillusioned
with the Labour party. As with the Liberal radicals in the 1880s and 1890s, it
was widely felt that the party had other priorities.*

As a rule, Socialists are silent on the question of women. If not actually antagonistic to the movement for women's rights, they hold aloof from it. One
gathers that, some day, when the Socialists are in power, and have nothing
better to do, they will give women votes as a finishing touch to their arrangements, but for the present they profess no interest in the subject. ... Why are
women expected to have such confidence in the men of the Labour Party?
Working-men are as unjust to women as are those of other classes.

Christabel Pankhurst, *ILP News*, August 1903, quoted in [114], pp. 28–9.

DOCUMENT 25   THE PARLIAMENT ACT 1911

*The main terms of the Parliament Act, which resolved the constitutional
impasse between Lords and Commons, are well enough known. Two important
facts are, however, worth stressing here. The two-year delay which the Lords
could impose on the Commons before legislation voted down in the upper
house became law did not apply to money bills. Secondly, the Liberals' intention
was to produce more radical legislation to fashion a second chamber with a
more 'popular' basis. Nothing came of this and no specific proposals were
presented. The same problem – not how to clip the Lords' wings but how to
agree on an alternative composition which downgraded, or eliminated, the
hereditary element – has still not been solved by a reformist Labour government at the very end of the twentieth century.*

An Act to make provision with respect to the powers of the House of Lords in relation to those of the House of Commons, and to limit the duration of parliament.

Whereas it is expedient that provision should be made for regulating the relations between the two Houses of parliament. And whereas it is intended to substitute for the House of Lords as it at present exists a second chamber constituted on a popular instead of a hereditary basis, but such substitution cannot be immediately brought into operation. ...

Be it therefore enacted: ... If a Money Bill, having been passed by the House of Commons, and sent up to the House of Lords at least one month before the end of the session, is not passed by the House of Lords without amendment within one month after it is so sent up to that House, the bill shall, unless the House of Commons direct to the contrary, be presented to his majesty and become an Act of parliament on the Royal Assent being signified, notwithstanding that the House of Lords have not consented to the bill. ...

If any Public Bill (other than a Money Bill or a bill containing any provision to extend the maximum duration of parliament beyond five years) is passed by the House of Commons in three successive sessions (whether of the same parliament or not) ... is rejected by the House of Lords in each of those sessions, that bill shall, on its rejection for the third time by the House of Lords, unless the House of Commons direct to the contrary, be presented to his majesty and become an Act of parliament on the Royal Assent being signified thereto, notwithstanding that the House of Lords shall not take effect until two years have elapsed between the date of the second reading in the first of those sessions of the bill in the House of Commons and the date on which it passes the House of Commons in the third of those sessions. ...

Five years shall be substituted for seven years as the time fixed for the maximum duration of parliament under the Septennial Act of 1715 [1716 in the new-style calendar].

Public General Statutes, 1 & 2 George V, cap. 13.

DOCUMENT 26   A SENIOR DOCTOR DOUBTS THE SANITY OF THE SUFFRAGETTES

Pronouncements about those intrinsic differences between men and women which rendered it inadvisable for the latter to have the vote were common in late nineteenth and early twentieth-century Britain. The following extract shows how far a basic premise could be pushed. It also uncannily presages charges made against feminism in the 1970s and 1980s. Its author was no wild eccentric but one of the most distinguished doctors of his day. Sir Almroth Wright (1861–1947) was a Professor of Pathology, pioneered anti-typhoid inoculation and did distinguished research on war wounds during the First World War. Notice the assumption that unmarried women were 'excess ... population', without a proper role.

For man the physiology and psychology of woman is full of difficulties. He is not a little mystified when he encounters in her periodically recurring phases of hypersensitiveness, unreasonableness, and loss of sense of proportion. ... No doctor can ever lose sight of the fact that the mind of woman is always threatened with danger from the reverberations of her physiological emergencies. It is with such thoughts that the doctor lets his eyes rest upon the militant suffragist. He cannot shut them to the fact that there is mixed up with the women's movement much mental disorder. ... The recruiting field for the militant suffragists is the half million of our excess female population – that half million which had better long ago have gone to mate with its complement of men beyond the seas.

If women's suffrage comes in here, it will have come as a surprise to a very violent feminist agitation – an agitation which we have traced back to our excess female population and the assorted abnormal physiological conditions. If ever parliament concedes the vote to women in England, it will not be accepted by the militant suffragist as an eirenicon [peace offering], but as a victory which she will value only for the better carrying out her fight ... against the oppression and injustice of men.

Letter to *The Times*, 28 March 1912, quoted in [4], pp. 184–5.

DOCUMENT 27   SUFFRAGETTES STEREOTYPED

This article from a popular newspaper was typical of many which argued that suffragettes had become hopelessly embittered and were unable to think straight. The strong implication is that, by 1914, they were so embattled that they were likely to see even moderate supporters of franchise extension as sworn enemies.

There is no longer any need for the militants to wear their colours or their badges. Fanaticism has set its seal upon their faces and left a peculiar expression which cannot be mistaken. Nowadays, indeed, any observant person can pick out a suffragette in a crowd of other women. They have nursed a grievance for so long that they seem resentful of anyone who is happy and contented and appear to be exceptionally bitter against the members of their own sex who do not support their policy of outrage.

Daily Mirror, 25 May 1914.

DOCUMENT 28   A SUFFRAGETTE EXPLAINS HER REASONS
FOR THE TRUCE WITH THE
GOVERNMENT

The First World War brought the accelerating suffragette campaign of disruption, violence and arson to almost a complete halt. The following extract, from Christabel Pankhurst, explains why. It indicates how prevalent was anti-Germanism across the political spectrum and how readily leading supporters of the women's campaign put aside domestic struggle in the interests of patriotism.

... the success of the Germans would be disastrous for the civilisation of the world, let alone for the British Empire. All – everything – that we women have been fighting for and treasure would disappear in the event of a German victory. The Germans are playing the part of savages, over-riding every principle of humanity and morality, and taking us back to the manners and methods of the dark ages. ... Among certain people there is a sort of idea that present events form part of evolution – that it is ordained that Germany shall supplant England. We suffragists ... do not feel that Great Britain is in any way decadent. On the contrary, we are tremendously conscious of strength and freshness.

Christabel Pankhurst, *Daily Telegraph*, 4 September 1914, quoted in [114], pp. 249–50.

DOCUMENT 29   THE HOME SECRETARY INTRODUCES THE
REPRESENTATION OF THE PEOPLE BILL

The First World War changed perspectives on representation in the most radical way. Contemporaries, and many historians since, argued that the collective effort involved in fighting war on such a massive scale – not least conscription into military service which was introduced in 1916 – overbore most of the resistance to universal franchise. The speech here refers to the relative triviality of 'class divisions'. The reference to the absence of 'civil turmoil' was also intended to convince MPs that Britain was somehow special, although by this time its franchise was remarkably restrictive in comparison with other European countries. The Home Secretary, Sir George Cave (1856–1928), was a barrister and had been Unionist MP for Kingston since 1906. He had been Solicitor General under Asquith's coalition government before being promoted by Lloyd George.

For these [qualifications from 1884], the Bill proposes to substitute three alternative qualifications only. The first is the qualification of residence, which obviously includes not only householders, the lodgers and the service voters, but also a certain number of residents qualified by age to vote, who are not in any existing class of voters. Secondly, the occupation of business premises of annual value of £10, and thirdly the university vote, which is enlarged by the inclusion of all the graduates. ...

We have seen since 1832 that the addition of new classes of our fellow countrymen to a share in the government of their country makes for contentment and stability. It frees this country from the civil turmoil which we have seen during that period in almost every country in Europe, and adds strength to the throne. ... I think this feeling has been strengthened by recent events. The spirit manifested in this War by all classes of our countrymen has brought us nearer together, has opened men's eyes, and removed misunderstandings on all sides. It has made it, I think, impossible that ever again, at all events in the lifetime of the present generation, there should be a revival of the old class feeling which was responsible for so much, and, among other things, for the exclusion for a period of so many of our population from the class of electors. I think I need say no more to justify this extension of the franchise.

I pass to a much more thorny subject. ... The qualifications proposed for women are different from the qualifications for men. ... The Bill imposes an age limit for women. Of the two ages which found favour with the [Speaker's] Conference we have taken the age of thirty in preference to thirty-five, an age which would shut women out from the franchise for one half the allotted span of life. The other qualifications are: (1) The woman voter must be entitled to be registered as a local government elector, or (2) she must be the wife of a husband so entitled, or (3) she must be a university voter. It is estimated that this provision will add to the register about 6,000,000 voters, of whom 5,000,000 will come on as married women.

Sir George Cave, House of Commons, 22 May 1917, *Hansard*, 5th series, vol. 93, cols 2134–5.

DOCUMENT 30   **DEBATES ON THE ADVISABILITY OF ENFRANCHISING WOMEN**

The First World War greatly reduced contention among MPs over women's suffrage. This contribution to the debate on the Representation of the People Act by Cecil Cochrane (1869–1960) advances the arguments most typically brought forward. He stresses women's selfless sacrifice and, importantly, their abandonment of militancy. Cochrane was a Liberal MP from the north-east who represented South Shields from 1916 to 1918. He was a director of several mining and industrial companies. Reginald Blair (1881–1962), who maintained a strong anti-woman's franchise stance until the end, had defeated the Labour MP George Lansbury at a famous by-election in 1912 after Lansbury had resigned his east London seat of Bromley and Bow. Lansbury's purpose had been to offer himself for re-election as an independent Labour candidate on the specific issue of votes for women. Blair defeated him by 751 votes. Blair's subsequent parliamentary career was long (he was MP from 1912 to

*1922 and then from 1935 to 1945) but not distinguished. His love for the turf
exceeded that of politics and he was Chairman of the Racecourse Betting
Control Board.*

MR COCHRANE: In my opinion the case for the extension of the franchise to
women has been enormously strengthened during the last three years. I venture
to attribute that change of feeling to two main causes. In the first place, it is
due to the conspicuous services that women have rendered to the nation during
the War. Their perseverance, their energy, their adaptability, and their
resources, have surpassed anything that I think anyone imagined as possible.
... I think the House will agree, that it would have been impossible to have
carried the War without them. The second change which has contributed to
this change of feeling, I suggest, is the total abstinence from those militant
methods which, I believe, did far more damage to their cause than their
strongest opponents ever realised. ... I believe the unanimity with which the
proposals of this Bill have been received throughout the country during the
time since this Bill has been made public affords marvellous evidence of its
popularity.

MR BLAIR: I oppose the Second Reading of this Bill. ... I frankly confess that in
France I have met many soldiers who have changed their opinions, but I
regret to say that they have always given their reasons for change as a reward
for the great and noble services that women have given in this terrible war.
Personally, I think that to talk about giving the vote as a reward to women is
an insulting proposal. If you are going to give it as a reward for their services,
I should like to ask what reward are you going to give to the 1,250,000 young
men between the ages of fourteen and eighteen who, we are told by the Minister of Munitions, have been gallantly carrying on their own shoulders some
of the burdens of this War. ... Are you going to give the same vote to a soldier
as to the lady of thirty years of age who has worked very hard in a munitions
factory or in a canteen kitchen? ... I challenge hon. Members who have served
in France to say that they have ever heard in France the cry of 'Votes for
Women'. ... I should be ashamed to go back to France and tell these French-
women that although my sisters in England had done so nobly in this War,
that they had, in the middle of this great War, demanded that they should be
given the vote.

Cecil Cochrane and Reginald Blair, House of Commons, 22 May 1917, *Hansard*,
5th series, vol. 93, cols 2207–8, 2215–16.

CHRONOLOGY

1768–69   John Wilkes's campaign to take his seat as the elected MP for Middlesex stimulates much popular support and revives the issue of parliamentary reform.

1769   'Bill of Rights Society' founded to support Wilkes.

1771   Bill of Rights Society passes resolutions in favour of parliamentary reform, including annual parliaments. MP John Sawbridge presents the first of many yearly motions to have the life of parliament limited to one year.

1776   Major John Cartwright's pamphlet *Take Your Choice* advocates universal manhood suffrage and other key parliamentary reforms. Wilkes fails to find a seconder in the Commons for his motion on parliamentary reform.

1779   Rev Christopher Wyvill forms the 'Yorkshire Association' to support reform in government.

1780   John Cartwright and John Jebb form the Society for Constitutional Information, joined by many who had supported the Wilkes campaigns.

1781   Westminster Association petition for parliamentary reform rejected by the Commons (212–135).

1782   Younger Pitt's Commons resolution to consider parliamentary reform defeated (161–141).

1783   Younger Pitt's reform bill to increase number of members for counties and larger boroughs defeated in Commons (293–149).

1785   Pitt's presented bill for parliamentary reform as prime minister to buy out 36 small boroughs and transfer their MPs to counties and London. Defeated in Commons (248–174).

1789   Outbreak of French Revolution.

1790   Burke attacks the revolution in *Reflections on the Revolution in France.*

1791   Part I of Tom Paine's *Rights of Man* published. Sheffield Society for Constitutional Information founded: the first artisan society of the period.

1792   Part II of *Rights of Man* published. The whole book declared a seditious libel by the government. London Corresponding Society and Whig Association of the Friends of the People formed.

1793   Beginning of French Wars. Charles Grey's resolution to consider parliamentary reform rejected by Commons (282–41). Trials of radicals for sedition begin in Scotland.

1794   Habeas Corpus amendment Act passed. Trial of leading members of the London Corresponding Society.

1795   Widespread economic distress increases support for parliamentary reform. Pitt's government passes the Treasonable Practices and Seditious Meetings Act. Much radical activity soon suppressed. Some underground revolutionary activity begins.

1797   Mutinies in the navy: evidence of radical activity in at least one of them. Grey's bill for parliamentary reform presented. It includes proposals to give votes to copyholders in counties and to householders in boroughs. Defeated (248–174).

1798   Government increases taxes on newspapers in an attempt to drive radical publications out of existence. Habeas Corpus suspended.

1799   London Corresponding Society formally banned along with other 'seditious and treasonable societies'. Passage of Combination Acts confirming illegality of trade unions.

1800   Act of Union creates a number of new parliamentary constituencies in Ireland: 64 county, 35 borough and one university seat created as Irish representation in the UK parliament.

1801   During another period of economic distress, Habeas Corpus suspended again.

1803   Revolutionary Despard conspiracy involving 'United Irishmen' and 'United Englishmen' discovered; Despard executed.

1807	The election of Sir Francis Burdett and Lord Cochrane for Westminster as radical candidates against both Whigs and Tories helps to revive the reform issue.
1808	Leigh Hunt's journal *The Examiner* founded to revive the parliamentary reform issue.
1809	Burdett's motion to consider parliamentary reform defeated in the Commons (74–15).
1810	Thomas Brand introduces a bill to give the vote to householders in the boroughs and to extend it to copyholders in the counties, to disfranchise small boroughs and to restrict life of parliament to three years. Defeated (234–115).
1811	John Cartwright forms a new 'Union for Parliamentary Reform'.
1812	First meeting of Cartwright's Hampden Club calling for parliamentary reform and a householder franchise. Luddite activities include some support for reform.
1813	Cartwright begins his 'missionary' tours to convert provinces to the reform cause.
1815	End of French Wars followed by widespread economic depression. Liverpool's government passes a new protectionist Corn Law.
1816	Major reform meetings in Spa Fields, London. Hampden Clubs formed in many northern towns.
1817	Habeas Corpus suspended; new Act banning seditious meetings. Pentrich rising in Derbyshire.
1818	Jeremy Bentham produces a pamphlet on parliamentary reform.
1819	Economic distress helps to increase radical activity. 'Peterloo massacre' excites widespread revulsion. Government passes 'Six Acts'.
1820	Cato Street conspiracy to murder the Cabinet exposed; its leaders executed. Queen Caroline divorce scandal polarises society; most reformers support the Queen.
1822	Lord John Russell's motion to remove one seat from the hundred smallest parliamentary boroughs and redistribute them to the counties and largest towns. Defeated (269–164).

1826   Borough of Grampound (Cornwall) disfranchised for corruption; its two seats added to Yorkshire, England's largest county.

1829   Roman Catholic emancipation enables Catholics to become MPs. Tory government increases county voting qualification from 40s. (£2) to £10 to stop Irish Catholic peasantry from voting *en masse* for Catholic candidates. County voters reduced from 216,000 to about 37,000 as a result.

1830   *February*: the ultra Tory Blandford's parliamentary reform bill defeated (160–57).
        February: Russell's bill to give direct representation to Birmingham, Leeds and Manchester defeated (188–140).
        May: Daniel O'Connell bill for universal manhood suffrage, secret ballot, triennial parliaments defeated (319–13).
        May: Russell's proposal to take away 60 seats from smallest boroughs (with compensation to owners) and transfer them to biggest towns and most populated counties defeated (213–117).
        June: death of George IV necessitates a general election in which Tories suffer losses.
        November: Wellington declares that current state of representation has the confidence of the country and is forced to resign soon after. Grey forms a Whig-dominated coalition government with some 'liberal' Tories, pledged to reform.

1831   *March*: Government reform bill passed in Commons by single vote (302–301).
        April: Grey asks for, and receives, dissolution of parliament after government defeat on detail of the bill. Subsequent election gives government strong pro-reform majority.
        July: reform bill passes in Commons with large majority (367–231).
        October: reform bill rejected by Lords (199–158); widespread rioting ensues.
        December: further bill presented and passes Commons by huge majority (324–162).

1832   *January*: William IV agrees to create extra peers, if necessary, to get a majority for the reform bill.
        April: bill passes in Lords (184–175).
        May: Government defeated in Lords on a Tory amendment (151–116). Grey calls on King to create 50–60 peers immediately. When he refuses, Grey resigns. Wellington tries to form government but fails. Grey invited back, the King now promising to create as many peers as required.

June: Lords back down with peerage creations. Bill passed there (106–22) and receives royal assent. Separate bills also for Scotland and Ireland.

1836   London Working Men's Association formed to press for radical reform.

1837   Lord John Russell declares the Reform Act a 'final solution' to the constitutional issue.

1838   People's Charter, with six 'democratic' points, published.

1839   Chartist petition rejected by Commons (235–46).

1842   Commons refuses to consider second Chartist petition (287–49), leading to strikes and widespread unrest.

1848   Large Chartist convention. The authorities refuse to allow mass Chartist march to accompany delivery of a further petition for democratic reforms. Russell announces that he does not believe the 1832 settlement to be 'final'.

1849   Formation of National Parliamentary and Financial Reform Association, led by Joseph Hume and Joshua Walmsley, calling for equal electoral districts.

1850   Irish Franchise Act passed because of disastrous demographic effects of the Famine. The 'certification' system, which had restricted the electorate, abandoned and a new qualification based on occupation of property introduced.

1852   Russell introduces bill to extend vote to householders with rental value of £5 in the boroughs and £20 in the counties but his government falls before it can be concluded.

1853   Formation of Ballot Society, chaired by F.H.F. Berkeley, to campaign for the secret ballot.

1854   Russell bill to extend vote to £6 householders in boroughs and £10 in counties, and to disfranchise certain small boroughs, transferring their seats to counties and boroughs, withdrawn on outbreak of Crimean War.
        Russell's Act on bribery provides the first workable definitions of bribery and 'treating' and prescribes fines for misdemeanour. Election accounts also have to be kept. It has limited effectiveness.

1858   The requirement for MPs to own property of a certain value abolished.

1859   Extensive bill introduced by Derby's minority Conservative government: a uniform £10 borough and county franchise and a £20 lodger franchise proposed, together with redistribution of seats, mainly to the counties. Also proposes votes for members of professions, university graduates etc. – the so-called 'fancy franchises'. Defeated (330–291), leading to a dissolution of parliament and return of Liberals to office.

1860   Russell's bill to extend vote to £6 borough and £10 county householders, together with redistribution of seats. Withdrawn after evidence of backbencher hostility.

1864   Largely middle-class Reform Union founded in Manchester to press for further parliamentary reform. Its membership similar to that which had campaigned for the repeal of the Corn Laws. Gladstone announces his conversion to an increased franchise in speech to parliament.

1865   Reform League founded, largely supported by skilled working classes but with substantial middle-class financial support. Death of Palmerston puts reform higher up the political agenda.

1866   Liberal Reform Bill proposed lowering franchise to £7 in boroughs and to £14 in the counties, with votes also for £10 lodgers and those with £50 deposits in savings banks. Minor redistribution of seats proposed: no actual disfranchisement but eight small boroughs to lose one seat and 63 to be grouped together to return 22 MPs. Most redistribution to go to the counties, with 26 extra seats. Six entirely new boroughs proposed with four more seats for London, five more for large English and three more for large Scottish boroughs. Government defeated (315–304) in the Commons on a hostile amendment, leading to fall of government. Derby forms a minority Conservative government.

1867   Derby and Disraeli's reform bill, much amended in its passage through parliament, reaches the statute book as the Second Reform Act. John Stuart Mill speaks in favour of women's suffrage.

1868   Reform Act (Scotland) passed, on same basic principles as that of England.
        Disraeli's government passes the Election Petitions and Corrupt Practices at Elections Act which transfers the hearing of allegations for corruption from the Commons to a judge. It has little effect on the volume of corruption.

In first general election since the Reform Acts, Gladstone's Liberal party defeats Disraeli and the Tories.

1869   Municipal Franchise Act gives votes in local elections to all who pay rates, whether directly or indirectly. Women ratepayers enfranchised on the same terms as men.

Goschen's Poor Rate Assessment and Collection Act has important franchise implications, since it restores compounding. Tenants now listed as rated occupiers, and thus liable to appear on the voting register.

1872   Gladstone's first government introduces a secret ballot for parliamentary elections.

Legal judgement restricts voting rights in boroughs to unmarried women or widows.

1874   First working men, Alexander MacDonald and Thomas Burt, elected to parliament, supporting the Liberal party.

1878   Dilke's Parliamentary and Municipal Registration Act makes clear that a person who rents a single room within a larger house, if that room is for separate occupation, is entitled to be registered as a voter.

1879   Elections and Corrupt Practices Act passed by the Conservatives, sponsored by Sir John Holker. Petitions concerning malpractice will be determined by two judges.

1880   An amendment to the 1879 Act removes restrictions on 'conveyance' of voters to polling stations in boroughs. This increases opportunities for election expenditure.

1881   Gladstone introduces a Corrupt and Illegal Practices Prevention Act but it fails to reach the statute book.

1883   Corrupt and Illegal Practices Prevention Act passed.

1884   Third Reform Act equalises voting qualifications in county and borough constituencies.

1885   Redistribution of Seats Act begins the process of reducing the discrepancy between the number of electors in constituencies. It also introduces single-member constituencies in most places. Opportunities for property owners to vote in more than one constituency are increased.

1888	Creation of County Councils. Women vote on the same terms as men.

1894   Parish and Rural District Councils Act passed. Women vote on same terms as men and can also stand as candidates.

1906   House of Lords rejects bills presented by the Liberal government and passed by large majorities in the Commons.

1907   John Burns's bill enables women to stand as candidates in municipal and county council elections.

1908–11 'Conciliation Bills' (so-called because they enjoy a measure of support across political parties) in favour of restricted women's suffrage win majorities in the House of Commons.

1909   Lloyd George's 'people's budget' is rejected by the House of Lords, thus provoking a constitutional crisis.

1911   Parliament Act reduces powers of the House of Lords (see Appendix I.)

1912   Asquith's Liberal government introduces Franchise and Redistribution Act. Its proposals would increase the number of male voters by up to three million.

1913   Speaker of the Commons rules that clauses to enfranchise women cannot be introduced into the Franchise and Redistribution Bill. Widespread suffragette militancy ensues.
         Government passes Prisoners (Temporary Discharge) Act. Nicknamed the 'Cat and Mouse' Act, it enabled suffragettes on hunger strike to be released on grounds of ill health but later to be rearrested and complete their sentences without any new trial being necessary.

1916   Speaker's Conference on the franchise established. It recommends (1917) universal male suffrage, votes for women and some proportional representation.

1918   Representation of the People Act (Fourth Reform Act) enfranchises nearly all men and most women over 30 years of age.

1928   Women receive the vote on the same terms as men.

1948   Representation of the People Act abolishes university constituencies and ends entitlement to plural voting.

1949   Parliament Act reduces House of Lords' delaying powers on non-finance bills from two years to one.

1958   Life Peerages Act enables people to be nominated to serve in the House of Lords on grounds of personal distinction or political nomination. They do not pass on membership of the Lords to their heirs.

1963   Peerage Act permits peers to renounce their title and, thus, to stand for membership of the House of Commons. The 14th Earl of Home does so months later in order to serve as prime minister, with the title Sir Alec Douglas Home.

1969   Representation of the People Act reduces voting age to 18.

APPENDIX I: PARLIAMENTARY REFORM LEGISLATION, 1832–1928

1 PARLIAMENTARY REFORM ACT (ENGLAND), 1832

Main terms

(a) 56 old boroughs were disfranchised entirely; 30 lost one of their two members.

(b) 22 new two-member and 20 new one-member borough constituencies were created.

(c) County redistribution gave Yorkshire six members; 26 large counties now had four MPs rather than two; the Isle of Wight was detached from Hampshire and returned one MP.

(d) In the counties, there were three main qualifications to vote:
   (i) adult males owning freehold property worth 40 shillings (£2)
   (ii) adult males with copyhold land worth £10 a year
   (iii) adult males renting land worth £50 a year.

(e) In the boroughs, the main qualifications were:
   (i) adult males owning or occupying property worth £10 a year, if they had been in possession of the property for at least one year, had paid all relevant taxes on it and had not received poor relief in the previous year
   (ii) adult males entitled to vote before 1832 could vote while they lived but could not pass their voting right on to their heirs.

(f) A register of voters was established in both borough and county seats.

Main franchise implications

Franchise increased by approximately 49 per cent. Approximately one adult male in five could vote after 1832. Redistribution of seats eliminated many of the 'rotten' or 'managed' boroughs, though much of the pre-1832 system survived. Some of the largest industrial centres, like Birmingham, Leeds and Sheffield, got direct representation for the first time. Many other sizeable towns were enfranchised for the first time. Overall, county seats increased from 80 to 144 and boroughs reduced from 405 to 323. Registration gave a fillip to electoral organisation by the Whig and Tory parties.

2 PARLIAMENTARY REFORM ACT (SCOTLAND), 1832

Main terms

(a) New basis for representation with election for 30 county (shire) members and 23 borough members:
   (i) each county to return one member, except that Elgin & Nairn, Ross & Cromarty and Clackmannan & Kinross grouped and returned one member each
   (ii) Edinburgh and Glasgow to return two members each; Aberdeen, Dundee, Greenock, Paisley, Perth to return one member each. Remaining 14 burgh seats elected from grouped districts.
(b) In the counties, there were two main qualifications to vote:
   (i) owners of property worth £10 a year
   (ii) leaseholders with leases over 57 years of property worth £10; leaseholders for 19 years whose property was worth £50; leaseholders who had paid £500 for their lease.
(c) In the boroughs, members now voted directly rather than voters being elected by town councils as before. The main qualification was occupation of property worth £10 a year, as in England.

Main franchise implications

Although the franchise remained very restricted, the increase in the number of voters from approximately 4,600 to 64,500 gave Scotland a semblance of a representative system for the first time. Approximately one inhabitant in 45 had the vote in the counties and one in 27 in the boroughs. Though the direct influence of the government's Scottish manager was greatly reduced, much corruption survived. Bad drafting made precise qualifications difficult to determine.

3 PARLIAMENTARY REFORM ACT (IRELAND), 1832

Main terms

(a) 32 Irish counties returned two MPs to the UK parliament, as had been the situation since the Act of Union (1800).
(b) Four new borough seats were added with additional members for Belfast, Galway, Limerick and Waterford; University of Dublin was given a second seat. Thus, total number of Irish seats rose from 100 to 105.
(c) In the counties, there were two main qualifications to vote:
   (i) owners of property worth £10 a year
   (ii) leaseholders to the value of £10, if leases were for 20 years or more.
(d) In the boroughs, there were three main qualifications to vote:
   (i) occupiers of property worth £10 a year
   (ii) in places designated 'counties of cities', owners and leaseholders of property worth £10 a year could vote
   (iii) adult males entitled to vote before 1832 could vote while they lived but could not pass their voting right on to their heirs.

Main franchise implications

The £10 ownership franchise (as opposed to 40 shillings in England and Wales) imposed in Ireland in 1829 as a result of Catholic Emancipation was sustained in 1832, but the addition of leaseholders increased the county franchise from 37,000 to 60,000. The borough franchise was about 29,000. The electorate was much more restricted than elsewhere in the United Kingdom. Only about one inhabitant in 116 was a voter in the counties and one in 26 in the boroughs.

4 IRISH FRANCHISE ACT, 1850

Main terms

(a) New system of maintaining voters' lists replaced the 1832 'Certification' system.

(b) Uniform qualification in counties and boroughs, which was based on occupation rather than ownership, related to poor law valuation and residence.

(c) Occupation value set at £12 a year.

Main franchise implications

Effects of the Famine had reduced total Irish electorate to about 45,000. This Act raised this to 135,000 in the counties and 28,000 in the boroughs.

5 REFORM ACT (ENGLAND & WALES), 1867 (SECOND REFORM ACT)

Main terms

(a) 38 post-1832 boroughs with populations of less than 10,000 lost one of their two members; four boroughs (Lancaster, Reigate, Totnes and Yarmouth) were disfranchised for corruption.

(b) Largest provincial cities (Birmingham, Leeds, Liverpool and Manchester) now returned three members rather than two.

(c) One new borough (Chelsea) was created with two new members; nine others were created with one new member each.

(d) From existing boroughs, Merthyr Tydfil and Salford received a second member. In London, Tower Hamlets was divided into two parliamentary boroughs, each with two members.

(e) In the counties, 13 new divisions were created, each with two members.

(f) The University of London was given one seat, now accompanying the two members each for the Universities of Cambridge and Oxford.

(g) In the boroughs, there were two main qualifications to vote:
   (i) inhabitant occupier of a dwelling house, if resident for at least 12 months
   (ii) lodgers occupying lodging houses worth at least £10 a year if resident for at least 12 months.

(h) By the so-called 'Minority Clause', in seats with three members, no elector could vote for more than two candidates; in seats with four members, no elector could vote for more than three candidates.

(i) In the counties, there were three main qualifications to vote:
  (i) owners (or lessees on 60 year leases or more) of property worth £5 a year
  (ii) occupiers of lands with rateable value of £12 a year, who had paid poor rates on the property
  (iii) those qualified under 1832 qualifications.

Main franchise implications

Electorate increased by approximately 90 per cent overall and more than doubled in the boroughs. The total electorate of England and Wales was approximately two million from a population of 22.5 million. In a number of the larger boroughs, working-class voters were in a majority. Political parties increased their organisation to appeal to new voters; party discipline was also extended. General elections were confirmed as the mechanism for determining the political composition of the government.

6 REFORM ACT (SCOTLAND), 1868

Main terms

(a) Glasgow's representation increased from two to three members (Minority clause operated as in England). Dundee's representation increased to three members.

(b) In the counties, Aberdeenshire, Ayrshire and Lanarkshire gained an extra seat but were divided into two single-member constituencies. Peebles & Selkirk were united to return one member; Hawick District was created with one member.

(c) Two university seats were created: Edinburgh & St Andrews (one member); Glasgow & Aberdeen (one member).

(d) Seven small-population boroughs in England – Arundel, Ashburton, Dartmouth, Honiton, Lyme Regis, Thetford and Wells – were disfranchised to make way for the new Scottish seats.

(e) In the boroughs, inhabitant occupier franchise as in England; lodger franchise also as in England.

(f) In the counties, ownership franchise as in England, but the occupation franchise was set at a rental of £14.

Main franchise implications

The number of voters increased substantially. By 1869, more than 230,000 voters were on the Scottish register, from a total population of about 3.3 million. The total number of Scottish seats increased to 60.

7 REFORM ACT (IRELAND), 1868

Main terms

(a) Franchise qualification in the boroughs was lowered to include occupiers of property worth 'over four pounds' a year.
(b) Vote in the boroughs was extended to lodgers.
(c) County franchise qualification was unchanged.
(d) There was some redistribution of voters from the counties to the boroughs.

Main franchise implications

In effect, Ireland retained a ratepayer, rather than a household, franchise unlike the rest of the United Kingdom. The number of urban voters increased from 30,955 to 45,625. The total electorate increased to approximately 230,000 from a population of approximately 4.5 million.

8 SECRET BALLOT ACT, 1872

Introduced a secret ballot in parliamentary elections. It was to run until 1880. Thereafter, its terms were annually renewed by parliament until made permanent by the Act of 1918.

9 CORRUPT AND ILLEGAL PRACTICES PREVENTION ACT, 1883

Main terms

(a) Bribery, treating, undue influence, assaulting, abducting or impersonating a voter were defined as 'corrupt practice'.
(b) Those convicted of corrupt practice were to be imprisoned and fined. Candidates were liable to perpetual exclusion from the constituency and exclusion from the House of Commons for seven years.
(c) Illegal practices were defined as exceeding maximum expenses or infringing a set of published rules on the use of election agents and proper rendering of election accounts.
(d) Those convicted of illegal practices were liable to fines and exclusion from voting rights and public offices for five years.
(e) Maximum allowable expenses were set for constituencies of different types.

10 PARLIAMENTARY REFORM ACT, 1884 (THIRD REFORM ACT)

Main terms

(a) Uniform household and lodger franchise was established in the counties and the boroughs throughout the United Kingdom.

(b) All adult males occupying land or tenements worth at least £10 a year were entitled to vote.

Main franchise implications

Throughout the United Kingdom the electorate increased from approximately 3.3 million to 5.7 million (72 per cent). The equalisation of franchise qualifications throughout the United Kingdom produced much the largest increase in Irish voters during the nineteenth century. The electorate there more than trebled: from 226,000 to 737,965. Approximately 65 per cent of adult males were entitled to vote.

11 REDISTRIBUTION ACT, 1885

(a) The first systematic attempt to relate parliamentary representation to population size. The work of redistribution was placed in the hands of politically neutral boundary commissioners.

(b) 81 parliamentary boroughs with small populations in England and Wales were disfranchised; two Scottish burgh districts were disfranchised; 22 Irish boroughs were disfranchised.

(c) Macclesfield and Sandwich were disfranchised for corruption.

(d) 21 English boroughs, one Welsh, one Scottish and one Irish still returned two members and voters exercised two votes. Elsewhere, single-member constituencies were established.

(e) The largest British cities had MPs broadly proportional to population: Liverpool had nine seats, Birmingham, Glasgow and the Tower Hamlets districts of London each had seven, Manchester six , Leeds five, Belfast, Bristol, Dublin and Edinburgh four each. Large boroughs were divided into single-member districts.

e) Radical redistribution of county seats; those with the largest populations were given the largest number of seats. Yorkshire was allocated 26 seats and Lancashire 23. All counties were divided into districts, each returning one member.

12 PARLIAMENT ACT, 1911

(a) The House of Lords' power to reject money bills sent to them from the House of Commons was ended.

(b) Lords could reject other legislation but not indefinitely. In practice, if the Commons persisted, the Lords lost the power to delay legislation for more than two years.

(c) Maximum length of parliament reduced from seven years to five. (Because of the outbreak of the First World War, however, the parliament elected in December 1910 lasted until November 1918.)

(d) Salaries (£400 a year) were paid for the first time to members of parliament who were not government ministers.

13 REPRESENTATION OF THE PEOPLE ACT, 1918 (FOURTH REFORM ACT)

Main terms

(a) Vote was extended in principle to all males over the age of 21 on the basis of residence. The residence qualification was reduced from one year to six months.

(b) Those who had served in the armed forces during the First World War could vote from the age of 19.

(c) Conscientious objectors who had not done war work as non-combatants were debarred from the franchise for five years.

(d) Rights of plural voting were curtailed. Now there were only two additional qualifications: occupation of business premises of £10 yearly value and status as a university graduate. Each qualified plural voter could exercise an additional vote only once.

(e) Votes given to women over the age of 30 if they satisfied one of three qualifications:
   (i) they were local government electors occupying property of £5 yearly value
   (ii) they occupied a dwelling house on the same basis as men who had been entitled to enfranchisement under the 1884 Reform Act
   (iii) they were married to a man entitled to be registered.

(f) Extensive redistribution of seats. The main intention, as in 1885, was to ensure that constituencies were of roughly equal size.

Main franchise implications

(a) The largest increase in the franchise in British history – from approximately 7.7 million voters to 21.4 million. In all four constituent countries of the United Kingdom the size of the electorate approximately trebled. [Note: the Government of Ireland Act restricted voters there to those in Northern Ireland after 1921, reducing Ireland's UK electorate from approximately 1.9 million to approximately 610,000.]

(b) About eight million women were enfranchised. The proportion of women voters in the electorate was approximately 40 per cent.

(c) The numbers of suburban seats and also seats dominated by voters who were workers in heavy industry were increased. The largest cities and towns also received more seats.

(d) The need for extensive political organisation in the constituencies increased. Overall the financial burden on the political parties increased.

14 EQUAL FRANCHISE ACT, 1928

Main term

Women over the age of 21 were enfranchised on the same terms as men.

Main franchise implications

(a) The size of the electorate increased from 21.7 million to 28.9 million.

(b) The proportion of women voters in the electorate was approximately 53 per cent.

APPENDIX II: THE GROWTH OF THE ELECTORATE AS A RESULT OF PARLIAMENTARY REFORM, 1831–1929

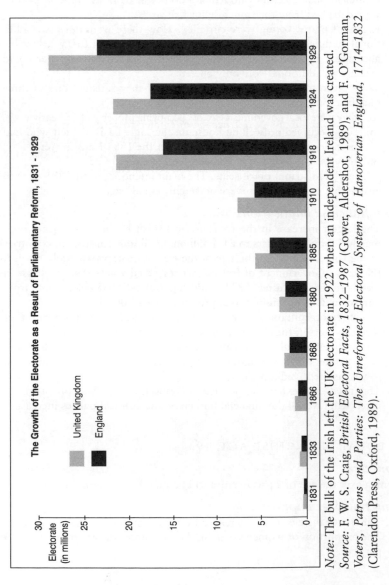

The Growth of the Electorate as a Result of Parliamentary Reform, 1831 - 1929

United Kingdom

England

Note: The bulk of the Irish left the UK electorate in 1922 when an independent Ireland was created. *Source:* F. W. S. Craig, *British Electoral Facts, 1832–1987* (Gower, Aldershot, 1989), and F. O'Gorman, *Voters, Patrons and Parties: The Unreformed Electoral System of Hanoverian England, 1714–1832* (Clarendon Press, Oxford, 1989).

BIBLIOGRAPHY

DOCUMENTS AND CONTEMPORARY SOURCES

That monumental series, *English Historical Documents* (Routledge), has three relevant volumes. Since it is heavily orientated towards the political and constitutional, it remains a useful quarry although now very creaky. Vol. XI, edited by A. Aspinall, covers the period 1783–1832. Vol. XII(I), edited by G. M. Young, the period 1833–74 and Vol. XII(II) edited by G. M. Young and W. D. Handcock the period 1874–1914. H. J. Hanham, *The Nineteeenth Century* (Cambridge University Press, 1969) is useful throughout but has a specially relevant section on 'The Franchise and the Electoral System'. E. A. Smith, *Reform or Revolution: A Diary of Reform in England, 1830–32*, Alan Sutton, Stroud, 1992 offers a wide collection of documents generated during the reform crisis of those years. An under-used collection of nineteenth-century sources is by J. B. Conacher, *The Emergence of Parliamentary Democracy in the Nineteenth Century* (John Wiley, New York, 1971).

SECONDARY SOURCES: BOOKS

Place of publication is London unless otherwise stated.
This is a select bibliography only. No attempt has been made to list all of the huge number of works which have been published on parliamentary reform. The choice here has been guided by the need to give advice to students wishing to pursue the topic in more detail. It is inevitably loaded and has been made in the knowledge that reference to additional books and articles with a narrower, or more specialist, focus are cited in recent monographs. Note that several of the works listed below are relevant outside the specific section to which they have been assigned. The selection – inevitably arbitrary in places – was made on the author's judgement of predominant utility.

General Works

1   Belchem, J., *Popular Radicalism in Nineteenth-century Britain*, Macmillan, Basingstoke, 1996.

2   Bentley, M., *Politics without Democracy, 1815–1914: Perception and Preoccupation in British Government*, 2nd edn, Fontana, 1996.

3   Briggs, A., *The Age of Improvement*, Longman, 1959 (now old but containing many still pertinent observations – new edition forthcoming).

4   Brooks, D., *The Age of Upheaval: Edwardian Politics, 1899–1914*, New Frontiers in History, Manchester University Press, Manchester, 1995 (contains a useful documentary section).

5   Eastwood, D., *Government and Community in the English Provinces, 1700–1870*, Macmillan, Basingstoke, 1997.

6   Evans, E. J. (ed.), *Social Policy, 1830–1914*, Routledge, 1978 (useful for tracing the changing social role of government as the electorate became more representative).

7   Evans, E. J., *The Forging of the Modern State: Early Industrial Britain, 1783–1870* 2nd edn, Addison Wesley Longman, 1996.

8   Gash, N., *Aristocracy and People, 1815–65*, Edward Arnold, 1979.

9   Gwyn, W. B., *Democracy and the Cost of Politics in Britain*, Athlone Press, 1962.

10 Hanham, H. J., *The Reformed Electoral System in Great Britain, 1832–1914*, Historical Association Pamphlet, 1969.

11 Hoppen, K. T., *The Mid-Victorian Generation, 1846–86*, Clarendon Press, Oxford 1998.

12 Hutchinson, I. G. C., *A Political History of Scotland 1832–1924: Parties, Elections and Issues*, Edinburgh University Press, Edinburgh, 1986.

13 Lawrence, J. and Taylor, M. (eds), *Party, State and Society: Electoral Behaviour in Britain since 1820*, Scolar Press, Aldershot, 1997 (see particularly essays by Taylor and Eastwood on the urban and rural electorates pre- and post-1832).

14 Lynch, M. (ed.), *Scotland: A New History*, Pimlico, 1992.

15 Parry, J., *The Rise and Fall of Liberal Government in Victorian Britain*, Cambridge University Press, Cambridge, 1993.

16 Pugh, M., *The Evolution of the British Electoral System, 1832–1987*, Historical Association Pamphlet, 1988.

17 Pugh, M., *The Making of British Politics, 1867–1939*, 2nd edn, Blackwell, Oxford, 1993.

18 Read, D., *Edwardian England*, Harrap, 1972.

19 Rubinstein, W. D., *Britain's Century: A Political and Social History 1815–1905*, Edward Arnold, 1998.

20 Seymour, C., *Electoral Reform in England and Wales*, David & Charles, Newton Abbot, 1970 reprint of 1915 edn.

21 Wright, D. G., *Popular Radicalism: The Working Class Experience, 1780–1880*, Longman, 1988.

The Background to Parliamentary Reform

22 Belchem, J., *'Orator' Hunt: Henry Hunt and English Working-Class Radicalism*, Clarendon Press, Oxford, 1985.
23 Brewer, J., *Party Ideology and Popular Politics at the Accession of George III*, Cambridge University Press, Cambridge, 1976.
24 Clark, J. C. D., *English Society, 1660–1832: Ideology, Social Structure and Political Practice during the Ancien Régime*, Cambridge University Press, Cambridge, 1985.
25 Derry, J. W., *From Luddism to the Reform Act*, Historical Association Pamphlet, Oxford, 1986.
26 Derry, J. W., *Politics in the Age of Fox, Pitt and Liverpool*, Macmillan, Basingstoke, 1990.
27 Dickinson, H. (ed.), *Britain and the French Revolution, 1789–1815*, Macmillan, Basingstoke, 1989.
28 Emsley, C., *British Society and the French Wars, 1793–1815*, Macmillan, Basingstoke, 1979.
29 Epstein, J., *Radical Expression: Political Language, Ritual, and Symbol in England, 1790–1850*, Oxford University Press, Oxford, 1994.
30 Evans, E. J., *Britain before the Reform Act: Religion and Society, 1815–32*, Seminar Studies in History, Longman, 1989.
31 Evans, E. J., *The Great Reform Act of 1832*, Lancaster Pamphlet, Routledge, 2nd edn, 1994.
32 Evans, E. J., *The Younger Pitt*, Lancaster Pamphlet, Routledge, 1999.
33 Harling, P., *The Waning of 'Old Corruption': The Politics of Economical Reform in Britain, 1779–1846*, Clarendon Press, Oxford, 1996.
34 Hobsbawm, E. J. and Rudé, G. F. E., *Captain Swing*, Penguin, Harmondsworth, 1969.
35 Hone, J. A., *For the Cause of Truth: Radicalism in London, 1796–1821*, Clarendon Press, Oxford, 1982.
36 Jupp, P. J., *British Politics on the Eve of Reform: The Duke of Wellington's Administration, 1828–30*, Macmillan, Basingstoke, 1998.
37 McWilliam, R., *Popular Politics in Nineteenth-Century England*, Historical Connections, Routledge, 1998 (very useful introduction to recent debates about radicalism and the nature of politics).
38 Namier, L., *The Structure of Politics at the Accession of George III*, 2nd edn, Macmillan, Basingstoke, 1982.
39 O'Gorman, F., *Voters, Patrons and Parties: The Unreformed Electorate of Hanoverian England, 1734–1832* Clarendon Press, Oxford, 1989.
40 Phillips, J. A., *Electoral Behaviour in Unreformed England: Plumpers, Splitters and Straights*, Princeton University Press, Princeton, NJ, 1982.
41 Rudé, G. F. E., *Wilkes and Liberty*, Oxford University Press, Oxford, 1962.
42 Sack, J. J., *From Jacobite to Conservative: Reaction and Orthodoxy in Britain, c. 1760–1832*, Cambridge University Press, Cambridge, 1993.

43   Thompson, E. P., *The Making of the English Working Class*, Penguin, Harmondsworth, 1968.
44   Veitch, G. S., *The Genesis of Parliamentary Reform*, Constable, 1913.
45   Wahrman, D., *Imagining the Middle Class: The Political Representation of Class in Britain, c. 1780–1840*, Cambridge University Press, Cambridge, 1995.
46   Worrall, D., *Radical Culture: Discourse, Resistance and Surveillance, 1790–1820*, Harvester, Hemel Hempstead, 1992.

The 'Great' Reform Act of 1832

47   Brock, M., *The Great Reform Act*, Cambridge University Press, Cambridge, 1973.
48   Butler, J. R. M., *The Passing of the Great Reform Bill*, Longman, 1914.
49   Cannon, J., *Parliamentary Reform, 1640–1832*, 2nd edn, Cambridge University Press, Cambridge, 1980.
50   Derry, J. W., *Charles, Earl Grey: Aristocratic Reformer*, Blackwell, Oxford, 1992.
51   Evans, E. J., *Sir Robert Peel: Statesmanship, Power and Party*, Lancaster Pamphlet, Routledge, 1991.
52   Gash, N., *Politics in the Age of Peel, 1830–1850*, Longman, 1953.
53   Gash, N., *Reaction and Reconstruction in English Politics, 1832–52*, Clarendon Press, Oxford, 1965.
54   Moore, D. C., *The Politics of Deference*, Harvester Wheatsheaf, Hassocks, Sussex, 1976.
55   Morris, R. J., *Class, Sect and Party: The Making of the British Middle Class: Leeds, 1820–50*, Manchester University Press, Manchester, 1990.
56   Phillips, J. A., *The Great Reform Bill in the Boroughs: English Electoral Behaviour, 1818–41*, Clarendon Press, Oxford, 1992.
57   Seymour, C., *Electoral Reform in England and Wales, 1832–1915*, Yale University Press, New Haven CT, 1915.
58   Smith, E. A., *Lord Grey, 1764–1845*, Clarendon Press, Oxford, 1990.

Between the Reform Acts

59   Biagini, E. F., *Liberty, Retrenchment and Reform: Popular Liberalism in the Age of Gladstone*, Cambridge University Press, Cambridge, 1992.
60   Evans, E. J., *Chartism*, 'History in Depth', Addison Wesley Longman, 1999.
61   Flick, C., *The Birmingham Political Union and the Movements for Reform in Britain, 1830–1839*, Dawson, Folkestone, 1978.
62   Hoppen, K. T., *Elections, Politics and Society in Ireland, 1832–1885*, Oxford University Press, Oxford, 1984.
63   Jones, G. S., *Languages of Class: Studies in Working-class History, 1832–1932*, Cambridge University Press, Cambridge, 1983.

64   Joyce, P., *Work, Society and Politics: The Culture of the Factory in Later Victorian England,* Harvester, Brighton, 1980.

65   Nossiter, T., *Influence, Opinion and Idioms in Reformed England: Case Studies from the North East,* Harvester, Brighton, 1975.

66   Prest, J., *Lord John Russell,* Macmillan, Basingstoke, 1972.

67   Royle, E., *Chartism,* 3rd edn, Seminar Studies in History, Addison Wesley Longman, 1996.

68   Shannon, R. T., *Gladstone, Volume One, 1809–65,* Methuen, 1982.

69   Stewart, R., *Party and Politics, 1830–1852,* Macmillan, Basingstoke, 1989.

70   Taylor, M., *The Decline of British Radicalism, 1847–60,* Clarendon Press, Oxford, 1995.

71   Vernon, J., *Politics and the People: A Study in English Political Culture, 1815–67,* Cambridge University Press, Cambridge, 1993.

72   Vincent, J., *Pollbooks: How Victorians Voted,* Cambridge University Press, Cambridge, 1967.

Reform, 1866–1914

73   Biagini, E. (ed.), *Citizenship and Community: Liberals, Radicals and Collective Identities in the British Isles, 1865–1931,* Cambridge University Press, Cambridge, 1996.

74   Biagini, E. F. and Reid, A. J. (eds), *Currents of Radicalism: Popular Radicalism, Organised Labour and Party Politics, 1850–1914,* Cambridge University Press, Cambridge, 1991.

75   Cowling, M., *1867: Disraeli, Gladstone and Revolution,* Cambridge University Press, Cambridge, 1967.

76   Feuchtwanger, E. J., *Disraeli, Democracy and the Tory Party: Conservative Leadership and Organisation after the Second Reform Bill,* Oxford University Press, Oxford, 1968.

77   Gourvish, T. and O'Day, A. (eds), *Later Victorian Britain, 1867–1900,* Problems in Focus, Macmillan, Basingstoke, 1988.

78   Hanham, H. J., *Elections and Party Management: Politics in the Time of Gladstone and Disraeli,* Longman, 1959.

79   Hayes, W. A., *The Background and Passage of the Third Reform Act,* Garland, New York, 1982.

80   Jones, A., *The Politics of Reform, 1884,* Cambridge University Press, Cambridge, 1972.

81   Kinzer, B., *The Ballot Question in Nineteenth-century English Politics,* Garland, New York, 1982.

82   Kirk, N., *Change, Continuity and Class: Labour in British Society, 1850–1920,* Manchester University Press, Manchester, 1998.

83   Lawrence, J., *Speaking for the People: Party, Language and Popular Politics in England, 1867–1914,* Cambridge University Press, Cambridge, 1998.

84   O'Leary, C. C., *The Elimination of Corrupt Practices in British Elections, 1868–1911*, Clarendon Press, Oxford, 1962.

85   Parry, J. P., *Democracy & Religion: Gladstone and the Liberal Party, 1867–1875*, Cambridge University Press, Cambridge, 1986.

86   Parry, J. P., *The Rise and Fall of Liberal Government in Victorian Britain*, Yale University Press, New Haven, CT, 1993.

87   Pelling, Henry, *Social Geography of British Elections, 1885–1910*, Macmillan, Basingstoke, 1967.

88   Pugh, M., *Electoral Reform in War and Peace, 1906–18*, Routledge, 1978.

89   Pugh, M., *The Tories and the People, 1880–1935*, Blackwell, Oxford, 1985.

90   Pugh, M., *State and Society: Britain 1870–1992*, Edward Arnold, 1994.

91   Shannon, R., *The Age of Disraeli, 1868–1881*, Longman, 1992.

92   Smith, F. B., *The Making of the Second Reform Bill*, Cambridge University Press, Cambridge, 1966.

93   Tanner, D., *Political Change and the Labour Party, 1900–1918*, Cambridge University Press, Cambridge, 1990.

94   Walton, J. K., *The Second Reform Act*, Lancaster Pamphlet, Routledge, 1983.

Votes for Women – and Many More Men, 1860–1918

95   Bartley, P., *Votes for Women, 1860–1928*, Access to History, Hodder & Stoughton, 1998.

96   Buckley, S., 'The family and the role of women', in A. O'Day (ed.), *The Edwardian Age*, Macmillan, Basingstoke, 1979.

97   Harrison, B., *Separate Spheres: The Opposition to Women's Suffrage in Britain*, Croom Helm, Beckenham, 1978.

98   Hollis, P., *Ladies Elect: Women in English Local Government, 1865–1914*, Clarendon Press, Oxford, 1987.

99   Holton, S., *Feminism and Democracy: Women's Suffrage and Reform Politics, 1900–1918*, Cambridge University Press, Cambridge, 1986.

100   Hume, L. P., *The National Union of Women's Suffrage Societies, 1897–1912*, Garland, New York, 1912.

101   Jalland, P., *Women, Marriage and Politics, 1860–1914*, Oxford University Press, Oxford, 1986.

102   John, A.V. and Eustance, C. (eds), *The Men's Share: Male Support and Women's Suffrage, 1890–1920*, Routledge, 1997.

103   Kent, S. K., *Sex and Suffrage in Britain, 1860–1914*, Princeton University Press, Princeton, NJ, 1987.

104   Kraditor, A., *The Ideas of the Woman's Suffrage Movement, 1890–1918*, Columbia University Press, NY, 1965.

105   Liddington, J., and Norris, J., *One Hand Tied Behind Us*, Virago, 1978.

106   Middleton, L. (ed.), *Women in the Labour Movement*, Croom Helm, Beckenham, 1977.

107 O'Day, A. (ed.), *The Edwardian Age*, Macmillan, Basingstoke, 1979.
108 Pugh, M., *Women's Suffrage in Britain, 1867–1928*, Historical Association Pamphlet, 1980.
109 Pugh, M., 'Labour and women's suffrage', in K. D. Brown (ed.), *The First Labour Party, 1906–14*, Croom Helm, Beckenham, 1985.
110 Pugh, M., *Women and the Women's Movement in Britain, 1914–59*, Macmillan, Basingstoke, 1992.
111 Pugh, M., 'The limits of liberalism: Liberals and women's suffrage, 1867–1914', in E. F. Biagini (ed.), *Citizenship and Community: Liberals, Radicals and Collective Identities in the British Isles, 1865–1931*, Cambridge University Press, Cambridge, 1996, pp. 45–65.
112 Ramsden, J., *The Age of Balfour and Baldwin, 1902–40*, Longman, 1978.
113 Rendel, M., 'The contribution of the Women's Labour League to the winning of the franchise', in L. Middleton (ed.), *Women in the Labour Movement*, Croom Helm, Beckenham, 1977.
114 Rosen, A., *Rise Up, Women! The Militant Campaign of the Women's Social and Political Union, 1903–14*, Routledge, 1974.
115 Rover, C., *Women's Suffrage and Party Politics in Britain, 1866–1914*, Routledge, 1967.
116 Rubinstein, D., *Before the Suffragettes: Women's Emancipation*, Harvester, Brighton, 1986.
117 Schwarzkopf, J., *Women in the Chartist Movement*, Macmillan, Basingstoke, 1991.
118 Smith, Harold, L., *The British Women's Suffrage Campaign, 1866–1928*, Seminar Studies in History, Addison Wesley Longman, 1998.
119 Searle, G.R., *The Liberal Party: Triumph and Disintegration, 1886–1929*, Macmillan, Basingstoke, 1992.
120 Tickner, L., *The Spectacle of Women: Imagery of the Suffrage Movement, 1907–14*, Chatto & Windus, 1987.
121 Walker, L., *The Women's Movement*, Lancaster Pamphlet, Routledge, 1999.

SECONDARY SOURCES: ARTICLES

The following abbreviations are used:
EHR *English Historical Review*
HJ *Historical Journal*
HR *Historical Research – previously BIHR (Bulletin of the Institute of Historical Research)*
IRSH *International Review of Social History*
JMH *Journal of Modern History*
P&P *Past and Present*
PH *Parliamentary History*
SH *Social History*

The Background to Parliamentary Reform

122   O'Gorman, F., 'The unreformed electorate of Hanoverian England: the mid-eighteenth century to the Reform Act of 1832', *SH*, 11, 1986, pp. 33–52.

The 'Great' Reform Act of 1832

123   Beales, D., 'The electorate before and after 1832: the right to vote and the opportunity', *PH*, 11, 1992, pp. 139–50.
124   Brash, J. I., 'The new Scottish county electors in 1832: an occupational analysis', *PH*, 15, 1996, pp. 120–39.
125   Ferguson, W., 'The Reform Act (Scotland) of 1832: intention and effect', *Scottish Historical Review*, 45, 1966, pp. 105–14.
126   Mitchell, L., 'Foxite politics and the Great Reform Bill', *EHR*, 108, 1993, pp. 338–64.
127   Moore, D. C., 'Concession or cure: the sociological premises of the first Reform Act', *HJ*, 9, 1966, pp. 34–59.
128   O'Gorman, F., 'The electorate before and after 1832', *PH*, 12, 1993, pp. 171–83.
129   Phillips, J. A., 'The many faces of reform: the reform bill and the electorate', *PH*, 1, 1982, pp. 115–35.
130   Quinault, R., 'The French Revolution of 1830 and parliamentary reform', *History*, 79, 1994, pp. 377–94.

Between the Reform Acts

131   Dyer, M., '"Mere detail and machinery": the Great Reform Act and the effects of redistribution on Scottish representation, *Scottish Historical Review*, 62, 1983, pp. 17–34.
132   Dyer, M., 'Burgh districts and the representation of Scotland, 1707–1983', *PH*, 15, 1996, pp. 287–307.
133   Gallagher, T. F., 'The Second Reform Movement, 1848–67', *Albion*, 12, 1980, pp. 147–63.
134   Hoppen, K. T., 'The franchise and electoral politics in England and Ireland, 1832–1885', *History*, 70, 1985, pp. 202–17.
135   Quinault, R., '1848 and parliamentary reform', *HJ*, 31, 1988, pp. 831–51.
136   Tholfsen, T. R., 'The transition to democracy in Victorian England', *ISRH*, 6, 1961, pp. 226–48.

Reform from 1867

137   Chadwick, M. E. J., 'The role of redistribution in the making of the Third Reform Act', *HJ*, 19, 1976, pp. 665–83.
138   Close, D. H., 'The collapse of resistance to democracy: Conservatives, adult suffrage and second chamber reform', *HJ*, 20, 1977, pp. 893–918.

139 Davis, J., 'Slums and the vote, 1867–90', *BIHR*, 64, 1991, pp. 375–88.
140 Davis, J. and Tanner, D., 'The borough franchise after 1867', *HR*, 69, 1996, pp. 306–27.
141 Dunbabin, J. P. J., 'Some implications of the 1885 British shift towards single-member constituencies', *EHR*, 109, 1994, pp. 89–100.
142 Garrard, J., 'Parties, members and voters after 1867', *HJ*, 20, 1977, pp. 145–63.
143 Greenall, R. L., 'Popular Conservatism in Salford 1868–1886', *Northern History*, 9, 1974, pp. 123–38.
144 Hoppen, K. T., 'Grammars of electoral violence in nineteenth-century England and Ireland', *EHR*, 109, 1994, pp. 597–620.
145 Hoppen, K. T., 'Roads to democracy: electioneering and corruption in nineteenth-century England and Ireland', *History*, 91, 1996, pp. 572–91.
146 Lawrence, J., 'Class and gender in the making of urban Toryism, 1880–1914', *EHR*, 108, 1993, pp. 629–52.
147 Lowe, J. C., 'The Tory triumph of 1868 in Blackburn and Lancashire', *HJ*, 1973, pp. 733–48.
148 Matthew, H., McKibbin, R. & Kay, J. A., 'The franchise factor in the rise of the Labour Party', *EHR*, 91, 1976, pp. 723–52.
149 Smith, F. B., '"Democracy" in the second reform debates', *Historical Studies*, 11, 1964, pp. 306–32.
150 Tanner, D., 'The parliamentary electoral system, the "Fourth" Reform Act and the rise of Labour in England and Wales', *BIHR*, 56, 1983, pp. 205–19.

Votes for Women

151 Hirshfield, C., 'Fractured faith: Liberal Party women and the suffrage issue in Britain, 1892–1914', *Gender and History*, 2, 1990, pp. 173–97.
152 Kent, S. K., 'The politics of sexual difference: World War I and the demise of British feminism', *Journal of British Studies*, 27, 1988, pp. 232–53.
153 Pugh, M., 'Politicians and the women's vote', *History*, 59, 1974, pp. 358–74.

INDEX